Breaking the Silence

The Untold Story

Steve Dickson
Autobiography

Author: Steve Dickson

ABN: 32643791182
Email: steve@stevedickson.com.au
Facebook: @SteveDicksonQLD

Copyright © 2020

First Published October 2020

The moral rights of the author have been asserted.

All rights reserved.

This book may not be reproduced in whole or in part, stored, posted on the internet or transmitted in any form or by any means, whether electronically, mechanically, or by photocopying, recording, sharing or any other means, without written permission from the author and publisher of the book. Please feel free to email me for permission, I'm usually obliging. All content found on or offline without written permission from me will be breaking the copyright law and therefore, render you liable and at risk of persecution.

ISBN: 978-0-6450035-9-8 (Paperback)
ISBN: 978-0-6450035-8-1 (ePub)
ISBN: 978-0-6450035-7-4 (Mobi)

Contents

Prologue..v

Chapter 1 – Humble beginnings...1
Chapter 2 – Into the big smoke..7
Chapter 3 – Working class..11
Chapter 4 – The expat..15
Chapter 5 – A backpacker's life..21
Chapter 6 – Outback adventures...27
Chapter 7 – Lucky in love...33
Chapter 8 – Digging for gold..37
Chapter 9 – Vows for life..41
Chapter 10 – The time of mince and sausages....................45
Chapter 11 – Our forever home...51
Chapter 12 – Throwing my hat in the ring..........................55
Chapter 13 – A promise made is a promise kept................59
Chapter 14 – Creative councillor...63
Chapter 15 – Memorable moments....................................67
Chapter 16 – Dipping my toe into the water......................71
Chapter 17 – Out of the pot and into the fire.....................75
Chapter 18 – The road to ruin...83
Chapter 19 – Pauline..87
Chapter 20 – Jumping ship..93
Chapter 21 – One Nation...97

Chapter 22 – The senate 105
Chapter 23 – The foreign agent 109
Chapter 24 – Setting the stage 115
Chapter 25 – The long haul 121
Chapter 26 – USA 125
Chapter 27 – The NRA 129
Chapter 28 – Big hitters and big business................................ 135
Chapter 29 – The set up... 141
Chapter 30 – Home sweet home 147
Chapter 31 – Al Jazeera.. 153
Chapter 32 – The smear campaign 161
Chapter 33 – The con 167
Chapter 34 – Crushed.. 173
Chapter 35 – The aftermath.. 179
Chapter 36 – The bitter pill... 185
Chapter 37 – Foreign interference.. 189
Chapter 38 – Recovery and research 197
Chapter 39 – The Covid campaign.. 201
Chapter 40 – Setting the record straight................................. 205
Chapter 41 – Bouncing back... 209
Chapter 42 – Reflection 217

Acknowledgments.. 219
Biography... 221

Prologue

A wave of sickness washed over me, mixing with the horror and realisation that not only was this manufactured mess being beamed into hundreds of thousands of homes around the country but it was also here in my home, on my TV. I looked over at my beautiful wife—my soul mate—and my amazing son, and everything inside me wanted to die . . .

Chapter 1

Humble beginnings

Australian politics were as far from my mind as the ocean, when I was a five-year-old, walking through the cow paddocks and small crops on my dad's dairy farm, with the Queensland summer breeze tousling my hair.

I grew up in the mining region of Gelobera on the Dawson Valley line, in the heart of beef country just outside Rockhampton. In 1962, I was the second child born on the farm to my dad, Lance Dickson, a farmer, and my mum Joan, a dental assistant.

My sister, Sandra, was five years older than I was and she was my mate as well as my protector as we played outside, rolled down banks into the marshmallow weed behind the dairy shed, and had a whole lot of fun on the farm. My younger sister, Teresa, didn't come along until nine years after I was born.

My great-grandfather, James, a Belfast-born engineer and gold miner, and his Queensland bride, Eliza, purchased the farm sometime in the 1890s. They drove a horse and dray from Cooktown to Gelobera, to begin their farming life, with their four sons, Dave, Dick, James and Lancelot (who became known as Pa), and their daughter Eva.

My grandfather, whom we called Pa, was a strong but fair man, who couldn't read or write until my grandmother (Ma) taught him how. He was a diligent learner and went on to serve as a councillor for 32 years in Mount Morgan, while still working the farm, cutting trees and even dabbling in bush poetry. My dad had two brothers and a sister; but, sadly, she died while still a toddler. My grandmother, Ethel (Ettie), had her work cut out with her tough boys. Jim the eldest, Ken in the middle and Lance (my Dad), also known as 'Ping', who was the youngest.

Jim was a typical country boy, physically fit and strong. During the Second World War, he was stationed in PNG, until he got malaria and had to return home to the farm to recover. After the war, he worked in the tourism industry and he and his mates were known to frequent Moreton Bay, where they water-skied and filmed their antics.  Being the powerhouse that he was, Jim used to lift women onto his shoulders and ski behind the boat with them sitting on his shoulders. He eventually settled down and married Robin, a world-champion squash player, after meeting her on a trip to England.

My dad tells the story of being flogged with a leather belt that had pennies stitched into it, by a brother at Rockhampton Grammar School. His legs were cut up and bleeding.

When Jim saw them, he immediately got in his car and drove the 50 miles back to Rockhampton, to confront the brother responsible. He grabbed him, threw him against the wall and said, "I've just come back from killing a whole lot of Japanese. One more life is not gonna make an ounce of difference to me! If you touch my brother again, remember what I've just told you".

Ken, the middle son, was old-school tough. He could ride, shoot, fight and he was smart. In the WW2, he served with a tank unit and the infantry, before becoming a fighter pilot. Ken wasn't home from the war long when he married his love, Ivy. They moved to Northgate in Brisbane, where he started working as a distribution manager and truck driver for a small company called Coca-Cola.

One day, his boss asked him to take care of a visiting executive from America, who was over here to promote Coca-Cola. Ken flew the man around the state visiting many country towns. On one flight, the plane had an engine malfunction and Ken had to perform an emergency crash landing. He used his fighter pilot skills and safely crash-landed, much to the executive's relief. He told Ken he owed him big time! Ken went on to become the managing director of Coca-Cola in Western Australia, and was awarded an MBE (Member of the Order of the British Empire) for his contribution to business.

Then, there was my dad, Lance, the youngest of the tribe. He was strong-willed, hard working, and had an energy level that kept everyone racing to keep up.

Dad was a good runner. He could run a mile in just over four minutes. In 1956, he was chosen to carry the Olympic torch just outside Rockhampton. Forty-four years later, I was chosen to carry the torch in Buderim. It was such an honour, not only carry the torch but also to follow in my father's footsteps.

Dad had two best mates at school; one was a bloke called John Black and the other was Rod Laver. When I was the Sports Minister in the Queensland government, John wrote to me recounting a story of how the three of them were playing marbles, when one accused the other of cheating. Not being able to work it out in a civil way, they decided to meet behind the school hall and sort it out the old-school way.

John Black, approached my dad and said, "I'm a bleeder. If he hits me in the nose, it's gonna go everywhere." Dad advised him, "Put your hands up in front of your face; that will stop him from hitting you in the nose." My father didn't want to see his two mates going at it, so he brokered a deal between them. Black was the best spin bowler on the cricket team, so he taught Rod how to spin a ball off a tennis racket—that was the deal, they were friends again!

Years later Rod went on to become the best tennis player in the world. I was fortunate enough to have had dinner with Rod and Roger Federer when I was the Queensland Sport Minister, in 2014.

As my great-grandparents got on in years, they shared farm duties and profits with my grandparents, who in turn came to the same arrangement in 1961, with my mum and dad. In 1963, Mum and Dad bought the farm outright from my grandparents, who moved off the land and headed to Redcliffe for a city change. Initially farm life was pretty tough for my parents, but they learned the ropes and worked hard, battling through the big drought that lasted from 1956 until 1968.

However, the drought was relentless and in 1965, Dad took a job on the railway line as a fettler—repairing the line between Gelobera and Dululu—to supplement the family income and to keep the farm going.

My dad was a fit and strong man, and stood at 5'10". He worked his heart out and tried everything to save our farm, which ran beef, milking cows, sheep, turkeys, bees and crops such as Lucerne, for ten years through the drought. He put down a couple of wells, but didn't have any success with them, so he had one last shot at digging into the core of the dehydrated creek we called Round Hole.

At the age of five, I had never seen rain. The creek beds were as dry as day old toast, but Dad took his tools, drove his tractor onto the creek bed and began digging. He worked at it for weeks, putting in a few hours each day, before jumping off the tractor, leaving the tools right there on the dusty creek bed and racing off to work on the railway line.

One day, Mum had just come in from looking after the sheep. About half a dozen had strayed onto the railway line and been hit. Mum had to get the survivors back on the path home, as she journeyed back to the farmhouse. She'd only just walked in, with me in tow, when the phone rang. It was Dad, casually asking Mum to go down to the Round Hole, to get the tractor out of the creek bed as there was a flash flood racing towards it.

Mum, who was the opposite of Dad, freaked out and ran wildly down the paddock with me flying after her to get our David Brown tractor out of the creek. I remember it as if it was yesterday. Mum jumped on the tractor and started it up, but it stalled right on the edge of the creek. Fortunately, Dad had had the foresight to call our neighbours, to ask them to help Mum. Young Errol Bunge—all 19 years of age—arrived on the family tractor, just in the nick of time. He hooked up a chain, towed us out and saved the day!

He was a good guy Errol, and I was happy when he ended up becoming my uncle, a few years later after he married my mum's sister. Sadly, he was taken way too early, passing on from a brain haemorrhage at the age of just twenty-two.

Flash floods are not a common occurrence out there. In fact, I'd never seen one before and I've not seen one since, so it is an event that has stuck with me. All of sudden, we could hear the water racing along the creek bed and towards Mum on the tractor. The wall of water would have been nine feet high and it was moving with such ferocity that it was capturing everything in its path—trees, bushes, sticks and all sorts of debris, which were swirling around in its belly, as it came flying at us like an inland tsunami.

From high up on the creek bank, I watched the wild water whip around and sweep Dad's tools up in its fury, never to be seen again. The flood disappeared almost as quickly as it had come; it drenched the creek and kept going past us downstream.

The only water we retained from the flood was a bit in the hole that Dad had been digging out, which did bugger all for our water supply or the thirsty crops.

About six months after the flash flood, Mum and Dad decided they'd had it with the struggle of farm life and the constant battle with the drought. Sadly, they announced that they had decided to sell the farm and move to Brisbane.

Mum and Dad sold the farm for $23,000, which was a lot of money in those days. On the morning of settlement, a frost came in and wiped out our Queensland Blue pumpkin crop, as well as several other crops in the area. I don't think I'd seen my dad so relieved that he didn't have to deal with that drama anymore.

I didn't realise it back then, but this time would have a big impact on my future, for my family and for me.

Chapter 2

Into the big smoke

In May 1968, we arrived in Carina, a small suburb, five miles drive from the Brisbane CBD. It was home to my family's new business venture—a 25-site caravan park that Dad and Uncle Jim had bought to run together.

It was a bit of a culture shock, at first. No wonder, we had exchanged a 3337-acre drought-ravaged bush property, which was more than ten minutes drive from the nearest neighbour, for a 33-acre South East Queensland property, which was lush and green and surrounded by houses, cars and people. However, the park delighted me no end as there was plenty of room for me to run and play, and there was peace and quiet, away from the hustle and bustle of the city.

Our new life began with Dad and Uncle Jim building toilet blocks and laying concrete pads for caravans, while Mum and Auntie Robyn rented out the caravans, ran the local shop and cleaned and looked after the amenities.

Sandra and I could walk to school, as it was only a 500-metre stroll away. Sandra was in Grade 5, and I was just starting out in Grade 1. I had a good teacher, who was a nice, caring, kind woman—she gave me a toy fire engine, which I loved. The highlight of my school days, every day, was meeting and playing with other kids.

Grade 2 rolled by, punctuated by the celebration for the first man's landing on the moon. I still remember us children being sent home from school, on July the 20th 1969, to watch the moon landing live on TV or, in our families' case, to listen to the live broadcast on the radio.

In Grade 3, I began to show some talent in sports and maths, both of which I loved. My years of running and jumping on the farm had been good groundwork and I found that I was naturally good at sports where I could do both, short and long-distance running, long jump, and high jump. I also excelled at shot put, cricket and rugby league, which I ended up playing for Queensland.

Reading and writing was another story, though. I really battled with them and they challenged me for most of my school life.

This caused me endless frustration and humiliation. My Grade 3 teacher was a real piece of work; a huge lump of a man, with a bad attitude. He turned my love of school into dread and he took great delight in being a mongrel. He was hardly encouraging on the best of days, but I remember one particular day, as I struggled to read a book called *Dick and Jane*, he said to me, "Follow my words, you are nothing but a f-----g idiot!" I'll never forget how dumb and ashamed I felt at that moment.

I never told my parents what he had said or how I felt about my academic problems. I was devastated and so embarrassed. I felt as if I had let them down somehow. Years later, I discovered I was dyslexic, and all my struggles suddenly made sense. I battled with it throughout my school years and eventually, I learned to cope with it and achieved what I needed to. In some ways, I think that teacher's words drove me to prove him wrong.

Although my grades in English were always low, my mathematics game was strong! I could crunch numbers easily—it all just made perfect sense to me. I also loved playing chess or anything else that had a bit of strategy to it. Anything that involved complex problem solving intrigued me.

I went to Carina State School until the end of Grade 3, and then my parents moved me to St Martin's Catholic Primary School, in the hope that I would get smarter. St Martin's was a great school, although the nuns were pretty tough. My Grade 4 teacher, Miss Kelly, only had one arm but she could do everything, and I really admired her.

Life in Carina was pretty good and I made quite a few friends: Dave Kells, Brett McGuinness, Kerry Dunne, Martin Nuttall and Tom Mosey, to name a few. Dave was the best man at my wedding and Brett was a groomsman, and to this day Dave and Kerry remain close mates.

I finished my schooling life at Coorparoo State High. My recollection of high school in the 70s is of girls and boys with long hair. Everybody was a music fan. We swam in creeks and streams; we rode our bikes everywhere and everyone joined in and loved the school sporting carnivals.

In fact, sport got me through high school. Most of my friends were teammates from footy—they were a great bunch of kids. Dave Kells and I looked forward to school finishing in the afternoons, when we'd eat left over plum pudding or wolf down a sandwich before heading off to football training. We were always hungry, because we were always active—my mother said we had hollow legs.

Other than the social side of school, I really liked woodwork and metalwork. I was also one of the first boys in Queensland to do home economics—cooking and sewing. I loved cooking, but sewing didn't interest me at all.

In those days, school was a hindrance to me; I just wanted to make money and play sport. I got real enjoyment out of helping people, and I especially liked to help the underdogs, as I hated any kind of injustice. I recall a boy at school, called Pope, who was a typical bully. He used to pick on all of the smaller kids, beat them up and take their lunch money. One day I got a bunch of my mates and we held Pope down, and we pierced his ear with a pen. We told him, "If you pick on anyone else we will do your nose next time."

What I lacked in knowledge, I made up for by being resourceful and asking enough questions to educate myself. I was determined to succeed, whatever it took. My great-grandfather, my Pa, my Dad and I all had the same ethos—give it all you got, take no bullshit and get the job done.

Chapter 3

Working class

Dad had gone from farmer to caravan park owner, but he wasn't satisfied with being just the latter. So, he bought a bulldozer and started hiring himself out to clear land around Brisbane, which had begun to really boom. As quickly as Dad cleared land, they had a concrete slab down, and houses were springing up all over the place. I used to go with him and learnt to drive the bulldozer—first parking it on the truck, then pushing trees over and clearing land.

My dad was my hero. One evening dad and his mate, Ralph Wildenberg, Mr W's son, John, and I went fishing for jewfish, at Lytton on the Brisbane River. Dad loved fishing, the peace and the thrill of the catch.

I was a scrawny kid of around twelve years old, who was loving sitting on the jetty with Dad on one side and Mr Wildenberg and John about thirty feet away on the other side. We'd been fishing for a couple of hours and had caught a few catfish and bream when a bunch of bikies turned up. They were big mean bastards, drunk and full of bad manners, the kind who would pick up a dead cat and throw it around just for fun.

They walked up the jetty, and made a beeline for old Mr Wildenberg. Straight away they began harassing him; pushing him around, swearing at him, and calling him a wog and a dog. Dad was the adult version of me, and he wasn't going to put up with an underdog being picked on. He told them, "Leave him alone!"

This didn't go down well with the bikies, and within seconds, two of them had grabbed Dad's arms and were holding him down. The leader came over and kicked Dad in the head. A gaping cut of about two inches long opened up and blood began to spill everywhere. However, Dad saw more red than was streaming from his head. He flicked the two blokes off his arms and jumped up. He punched the leader so hard in his gut that Dad's arm went all the way up to up to his elbow. I'm sure my eyes were as wide as saucers as I watched the guy jerk backwards and tumble off the jetty into the Brisbane River.

The tide was flowing quickly and some of the bikies jumped in after the leader who was floating away, while the rest ran away, not wanting to poke the bear any further. I'm sure he would have been happy to beat the living shit out of them all night, but no one was left. I knew my dad was a tough old bugger, but that night he rose even higher on my hero pedestal. This was proof (not that I needed any), that my passion for helping the underdog and my work ethic had come from a long line of strapping, hard-working, tough and determined men.

In my teens, I began to show the entrepreneurial streak that my dad and his forebears had had. I went out, created moneymaking opportunities and had a go at everything. My main goal was to buy my own car.

I learnt by doing and was ready to give any and everything a go. After I learned to drive the bulldozer at twelve, Mum and Dad confidently appointed me the caravan park's grounds person in charge of mowing, whipper snipping, pruning and weeding.

I also cleaned washing machines and emptied dryer fluff, everyday after school, for $10 a week.

I also made some money by selling Iced Vovo biscuits at school for 20 cents each. I had no overheads, as on those days I took a packet of Iced Vovos to school for lunch those days, from the caravan park shop.

We had a two-car garage at our house that I turned into the caravan park's entertainment area. A fella called Bob Alcock hired out washers and dryers to the caravan park, and I found out that he also had pinball machines and the like. Dad helped me out, and I ended up hiring three pinball machines, a jukebox and a pool table from which I got half the proceeds.

By this stage, the park had become one of the biggest in Queensland with 300 sites, and people everywhere, so I was pulling in about $30 a week. In addition to the entertainment area, I charged people 30 cents each to swim in our pool. In summer, I could have as many as 50 people crammed into the pool. It was busy and chaotic, but a whole lot of fun!

There were a lot of colourful characters around back then, and none more so than Malee, whom I met through my parents. Malee was a wild old man, out to make a quick buck, and who had his paws in just about everything. He was also known as 'Argus the Prophet' a fortune teller! He paid me $10 to put fortunes in envelopes, but every fortune was the same!

He was interested in caged birds and owned a pet centre that mainly sold birds. Every Saturday, my mum would drive me to Holland Park where I'd shoot sparrows with my trusty Daisy air rifle for most of the day. Malee paid me ten cents per head, to rid him of these pests. He also spent a fair amount of time painting sparrows yellow and selling them as canaries, which was great until it rained and the paint washed off, revealing the dirty brown sparrow!

Malee was also wrestling mad and he used to take me with him to the wrestling matches at Festival Hall, to watch the pros, such as 'killer' Karl Cox. I collected all of their signatures at the fighting ring, as Malee always got the best tickets and we'd usually be front and centre of each match. One day my sister, Sandra, got hit by a wrestler, who came flying out of the ring into our row of seats; poor Sandra went flying and copped a broken ankle!

I played poker a lot with the boys when it rained, which it seemed to do a lot in the school holidays. We started off playing for matchsticks, but quickly upped the ante and moved on to money. By the time I was thirteen, I had saved $4000 in $2 notes. I collected these notes in the hope of winning the radio competition where you won if they called out the serial number on your note. I never did win, but it wasn't easy to check 2000 notes!

In the summer of 1977, I was fifteen and I left school to begin my first paid job. I was a shop assistant at our caravan park, where I worked five days a week from 7am–6pm packing shelves, bagging potatoes and stacking the drink fridges, all for the princely wage of $40 a week, which was great for a fifteen-year-old fella.

I also got to go to the now-famous Rocklea Markets with Dad, to buy fruit and vegetables for the shop, along with stock from Tickles the Wholesalers. This huge store sold everything in large quantities. On one visit, Dad saw that toilet rolls were on special, so he bought enough to fill one of our garages to the roof. I learned what a bargain was, and how to take advantage of it to make a profit. This was a lesson that has helped me throughout my life.

Chapter 4

The expat

Things went a bit crazy in 1978, when Mum and Dad divorced. It was a terrible time for the whole family. None of us had seen it coming, but it seemed to be something they both agreed on. They leased the caravan park and each went off to do their own thing.

Mum ended up working for the people who had leased the caravan park and she bought her own little house for my sister, Teresa, and me.

Dad's mate, Graham, had the idea to start a pie shop in the Philippines. Dad thought it sounded like a good enough prospect, so he sold some of his treasures and pitched in some money to get the business started.

I had the choice to live with either Mum or Dad. I figured Teresa was keeping mum company, so I would go with the old man.

So, by the winter of 1978, Dad and I were on a plane bound for the Philippines—a new life in a new country. Arriving in Manila was a dead set culture shock. I'll never forget the first thing I saw in the street—someone cutting up a dog on what looked like a clothesline.

It took a while to adjust to my new life. Things were so different; people smashed concrete by hand, to get the steel reinforcing to sell for scrap metal—they did it tough! The Philippines were under martial law, and the control of President Ferdinand Marcos, at that time. The police and army had absolute control and could shoot you in the street if you resisted the president.

Graham took Dad and me to the Australia Club, a place where girls danced on the bar in bikinis. Initially I didn't know where to look and I was a bit embarrassed by it all. We sat down and the men grabbed some beers. I was never a big drinker; I'd have an occasional beer to look like the rest of the blokes, but that was about it. A girl came over and propositioned me. She just put her hands on me, and said, "Hey Joe, you want me? You pay me, I come with you." I wondered what the hell I'd gotten myself into!

We stayed in a hotel for two weeks, before we found a place to rent. Our new home was a unit in Manila and it was nothing flash. It had a couple of rooms, a bathroom and laundry and it was all that we needed.

Dad was a real go-getter and never one to waste an opportunity. While we were searching the country for things for the pie shop, we visited an island called Catanduanes, looking for gypsum, a mineral that Dad thought he might be able to export.

The Catanduanes people were very friendly. Some of the children had never seen a white man before and I quickly became a great source of entertainment, after I went for a bath in the creek. The kids laughed their heads off at the sight of me, "Look he's white all over!"

Dad and I had met a lot of weird and wonderful characters in the Philippines, and not just of the human variety. While wandering through a market in the Makati area I spotted a tiny, thin little creature looking sad and lonely in a cage. 'Mate', as he was quickly nicknamed, was a macaque monkey. He looked up at me with big, longing eyes, begging to be taken away from his caged life. Dad's heartstrings were tugged too, because he quickly took out his wallet and bought him, transferring ownership of the little fella to me.

Mate and I became great buddies. He was a funny little guy, who went everywhere with me, sitting on my shoulder and entertaining everyone with his antics. In many ways, he was like a rogue toddler. He'd get into all manner of strife so I had to keep him on a short lead (literally), otherwise he'd be into more than just cockroaches and fruit, which where his favourite things.

Dad and Graham were flat-out, brokering a deal to set up the pie shop in Makati, in metro Manila. Setting it up took months! Nothing was straightforward; permits had to be applied for, an oven had to be built, and all the equipment to fit the shop out had to be sourced or made. You couldn't just drive ten minutes with your shopping list to find what you needed. Instead, we had to travel the length of the country to get it.

Finally, after three months of working our butts off, Dad and Graham opened the doors to their new venture. Unfortunately, the excitement was short-lived. It seemed the Philippines weren't quite ready for the good old Aussie meat pie! Dad cut his losses and went looking for his next great venture.

While the demise of the pie shop was disappointing, it was great to be travelling again. I'm sure that in the time I lived in the Philippines I covered almost every square metre of it. When I wasn't working or helping Dad, I caught the train with friends and explored the country further. Public transport was antiquated in the Philippines and, on several occasions, I thought we were going to die travelling on the rickety train as it danced over the railway line.

One adventure brought me to a town called Angeles City. Here a friend showed me around and introduced me to her friends and family, who were all really lovely people. There's a lot to be said for travelling. It opens your eyes to cultures and ways of living that are foreign to us in Australia. The people I met and the homes I visited all made me realise just how lucky we were, and are.

The Filipinos didn't have much and lived very simply compared to us—but they were happy, and it was a humbling experience. Venturing through developing countries is something I have encouraged my sons to do, and I think all young people should do it at least once, to get some perspective and to gain a good lesson in gratitude and resourcefulness.

However, as with everywhere you go, there are some great people and some you would be better to avoid. In Manila, I made friends with a young bloke and we knocked around together for a while, until he stole my dad's gold and ruby ring shaped in a D for Dickson, along with some cash from our business. I never saw him again after that. It was a lesson I should have learned from, but I didn't. One of my shortcomings is trusting people too quickly and too easily.

After that, I mostly travelled around the provinces with Graham and Dad. The roads in the Philippines were bloody terrible and resembled the moon with their massive craters. The buses weren't much better. On one trip, I was so tired I lay on the floor at the back of the bus, with the chickens and piglets in cages, just to get some sleep, with feathers floating all around us. It could be crazy, but we always got a laugh out of the trips.

We met some beautiful people on our travels who always welcomed us with open arms and interesting stories. One group we stayed with made alcohol from their coconut trees. I didn't try it, but Dad and Graham did. Later on, I saw them filling their lighter with the same liquid—it must have been powerful stuff! The next day we were told if you drink too much of it you go blind; I was glad I didn't have any!

Dad's next venture was a hairdressing salon. Now, Dad wasn't any kind of hairdresser, but Graham's wife, Imelda, was. She had worked on selling Dad the idea, until he finally caved and purchased a salon she could manage, in Quezon City just outside of Manila, an area that was frequented by most of the movie stars.

Imelda was an experienced hairdresser so she knew the trade. Rather than hire someone, Dad and I worked the front desk taking the bookings and the money. This may sound odd but it was necessary. There was a lot of poverty in Manila and people constantly stole, to get money for things they needed. It was a sad state of affairs, but we couldn't trust anyone else to handle the takings, so it was up to Dad or me, to be there each day. If we weren't things would walk and money would mysteriously vanish.

I did my own thing on the days the salon wasn't open. I'd hang out with Dad or my friends. I was growing up and things were changing for me—I was nearly 17 and becoming a man. I'd discovered girls and there were plenty hanging around, who were intrigued because I was a foreigner. I met an attractive girl at the salon, Rona, and we started dating. She was a TV star who acted in a daytime soap, a bit like *Days of our Lives*. That definitely wouldn't have happened in Australia—a big TV star dating a lad like me! But, the Filipino girls loved Aussie guys who, like most young men, liked a bit of harmless fun.

It wasn't only us young guys, who got our fair share of dates; Dad did all right as well. In fact, he ended up meeting, dating and marrying a local woman called Cherrie, who had a young daughter. They stayed together for about ten years.

Although it was fun, the novelty of living abroad eventually began to wear off. I was over working in the salon and had become homesick. I missed my mum, my sisters and my mates back home. I broke the news to the old man and we arranged for me to head back to Australia. My little monkey, Mate, was left with Dad and Cherrie to look after.

Chapter 5

A backpacker's life

I arrived back on Aussie soil in 1979, just in time for Christmas. I stayed with my mum and Teresa in my mum's house in Birkdale, a suburb on the south side of Brisbane. It was fantastic to see them again and I realised just how much I had missed them. Mum was still working hard, running the office at the caravan park, and Teresa, who was now seven, was a couple of years into primary schooling and loving it.

I had a month catching up with family and friends and then I got straight into looking for work, before I went into the red. An ad for grape pickers in Mildura caught my eye and a few days later, my mate 'Kiwi' and I were heading to Victoria and the Delfaro Grape Farm in his XB Falcon.

Sam, the owner of the farm, was a great fellow. He gave Kiwi and me a room with a mattress each, and paid us 22 cents for each one-and-a-half-foot steel bin we filled with grapes. He also let me use his shotgun to shoot rabbits, which we cooked on the barbecue. I know it sounds a bit harsh eating a poor old bunny, but farmers in the area were grateful, as the rabbit population was out of control. They were causing havoc on the environment and the crops.

Rabbit warrens were like mines; you had to watch where you stepped or you could lose a foot.

Mildura was hot and dry. One afternoon we watched as a dust storm came through, bringing a wall of dirt at least a thousand feet high that blanketed everything in its path with muck. It was quite a sight.

We worked long hours during the week and let our hair down on weekends, going to the Working Man's Club in town, to play pool, have a drink and a laugh. That bar had to be the longest bar in the world; it was just over 298 feet long. After a beer and game of pool, we'd head to the dirt track motorbike races, just outside of town. One rider, Phil Crump, was a world champion and he was amazing to watch, as were the sidecar drivers in the races that followed the dirt bikes. These men were adrenalin junkies and so brave. It was a bloody dangerous sport and, sadly, many people were injured and even killed.

When the grape-picking season finished, about five months later, we packed up and headed to Shepparton, which was a couple of hours drive away. There we stayed with friends who owned a vineyard for a couple of days. Their place was a palace—everything in it was antique. It was an incredible, historical house and absolutely stunning. What a change for us, after spending five months on mattresses on the floor!

We explored Shepparton for a few days, before making our way to Melbourne, where we stayed with another friend we had met fruit picking. Then, after another couple of days, it was time to get back on the road again. We headed off to Canberra with Kiwi driving and me navigating. Neither of us had seen the place, but we'd both heard lots about it. I'd spotted what looked like a short cut on the map and, luckily, we had a full tank of fuel because instead of taking the left-hand turn, we took a right and ended up completely lost, in mountainous country, in the dark, bouncing over dirt roads that reminded me of the Philippines.

Our confidence that we would make it out the other side, in Kiwi's old XB, plummeted after we passed a broken-down, abandoned four-wheel drive. It was too late and too dark to turn around. We gingerly snaked our way through snow country as we watched the fuel gauge drop.

When we reached the top of the mountain, we pulled up for the night to get some sleep. The sunrise from the top of the mountain was spectacular and worth the trip, but we didn't hang around for long. Worried about our fuel supply, we were keen to get going and to find a petrol station, which we were fortunate to come upon before we'd used our last drop.

I have no idea how we managed to come out the other side of that mountain track and by all accounts, we shouldn't have. We both knew it and, as we cruised into the outskirts of Canberra, we thanked our lucky stars that Kiwi's old XB had held together.

My first impression of the nation's capital was how clean it was, almost to the point of sterility. The concrete-built city was spread out over a large area with wide vegetation-lined roads. There was a lot to see, but hardly any people walking around, which struck me as odd. Still, we had a great time doing all the touristy things, such as seeing Parliament House, Lake Burley Griffin, the embassies and the War Museum.

However, our time in Canberra finished with a minor brush with the law. After having a feed, we decided to get a few hours sleep before starting the long trip back to Queensland. The local coppers came across us sleeping and gave us the friendly 'move along boys' talk, which we took as our cue to get back on the road and we headed north.

After nearly six months away, we arrived back in Queensland just after my seventeenth birthday. I went back to Mum's in Birkdale.

I had just enough money left to buy the car I had always wanted—a 1978 Ford Cortina 250 4.1 litre V6. It was bright yellow with a brown vinyl roof; it didn't look like much, but man, could it go!

I'd spent all my savings, so it was time to look for work again. Gary Maguire, a mate I had played rugby league with, said there was a job going at his butcher's shop, if I'd like to give it a go. It turned out to be a great job; lots of fun and laughs with the boys, and I even learned how to make sausages!

There was always a prank on the go at Gary's and one day, they got me a beauty. They asked me to go to the bakery a few doors up from the butcher's shop, to get some pies and sausage rolls for lunch. Unbeknownst to me, the buggers had stuck a pig's eye on a piece of paper on my back that read, 'I've got my eye on you'. You had to put up with that sort of crap in those days. I can't imagine what the bakery staff thought when I turned around to walk out their door!

Gary and I hung out a lot outside of work too. He was still playing rugby league for Redlands and asked me to come and play, as they were short on players. It'd only been a year since my last game, so I wasn't too rusty and I have to say it was fantastic to get into sport again.

Winter came and went, the footy season ended and it was time to relax a bit. We'd sold a stack of raffle tickets over the season and the club was in such a good financial position that they had enough in the kitty to send us to New Caledonia for our end of year trip. We were so lucky; the club paid for the entire trip—airfares, transfers, and accommodation—for all the team.

The only thing we had to spot for was our food and drinks, and that's where we got creative. On the second day, we decided to check out the island's casino, which was in the Club Med resort, a 45-minute walk up the road. As we walked past the pool, the Club Med staff yelled out to us to come and play in their beach volleyball competition. We would have had a go without any incentive, but they went on to say that the winners of the competition would get free drinks and a free smorgasbord lunch, which was over and above their accommodation deal—within seconds we were on the beach warming up!

Being young, fit and fiercely competitive, we won every game and enjoyed the spoils of our victory. We went back again the next day, and the day after that, until they worked out we weren't guests at the resort and then the free ride was over, but we loved it while it lasted!

My youth felt like one great adventure after another. We lived life to the full and then some. How lucky we were to have the experiences we had. It wasn't lost on us, we knew it back then; we still know it today.

Chapter 6

Outback adventures

I had not been long back from the footy trip, when my grandmother called to ask me to help, at her sister's sheep station outside of Cobar in NSW. There had been an explosion in the number of feral pigs and they were killing the newborn lambs. I asked Gary to take the 1000km trip with me to cull the pigs and protect the lambs.

We spent a few days out there bringing the pig and kangaroo numbers down, before turning around and driving the 1000 km home. Just outside Cobar, we spotted an albino kangaroo in the bush. We should have taken it as an omen for caution, because just after midnight, as we crossed the border back into Queensland, I hit a big dip in the road going 100kph.

The Cortina's wheels locked up and we shot straight across the road, narrowly missing a semi-trailer that was heading in the opposite direction, before we careered headfirst towards a fence. We hit it hard and ripped apart one of the fence posts, the top of which came flying towards the windscreen, sliding and ripping up the bonnet as it hurtled towards me. I ducked, but not fast enough and the fence post hit me on the head, before it proceeded to tear into the roof, peeling it back like a can opener.

After the car came to a halt, everything was still and quiet, apart from Gary who had been jolted awake and was asking what the hell had happened.

I felt something warm running down my face and brushed it away. My hand came away red from the blood pouring from my injury.

We were both lucky to be alive. The driver of the truck we had nearly hit had acted quickly and called the police and an ambulance. We were taken to the Goondiwindi hospital, where the doctor stitched up my head wound with 32 stitches. Gary was very fortunate just to come away from the accident with bruised feet; I still have the scar as a reminder.

It was early 1982, and nothing was done in a hurry back then, so my mate, Martin Nuttall, suggested I head to the mines at Mt Isa, to do some work up there while I waited for my car to be fixed. My mate, Tony Boyd, was also keen to get work, so I finished up at the butchers and we caught a train from Brisbane to Townsville, and then another from Townsville to Mt Isa, to try our luck in the mines. It was a bloody long train ride, but I remember being served a mixed grill—it was the first time I'd had one, and I loved it!

The temperature was well into the 40s when we arrived at Mt Isa, and the flies buzzed around in their thousands. We stayed in a tent at the local caravan park, but we escaped it as often as we could to go to the library or the Irish Club, as they were both air-conditioned and fly-free. I tried to get a job in the mines for two weeks, without any luck, and my funds started to get dangerously low.

In the seventies, I'd met a guy at our caravan park called Malcolm Douglas. He told me a fantastic story about a place, located just outside of Darwin on the Anjo Peninsula, called the Truscott Airfield. Some years later, I saw a documentary by the now-famous Mr Douglas about the airbase and its Second World War history.

As I was having no luck finding work at Mt Isa, I decided to head to Darwin to look for work and visit to the airfield I'd heard so much about. Tony headed back to Brissy. Funnily enough, I never did get to visit that airfield.

The Northern Territory was in the middle of the wet season and many roads and areas were inaccessible, so I had to fly. It may have been called the wet season, but it was still as hot as a bastard. To escape the heat I went to the local pub, which I'd heard was rough and ready, with a reputation for its huge fights. I didn't much care about that, all I was interested in was getting a cold drink, and escaping the heat. We also all knew that if you wanted a job, you'd soon find someone at the pub who knew someone who had one on offer.

I struck up a conversation with a couple of local ringers[1*] who said there was work going at place called Elsey Station. I gave them a call and the manager said if I came out, they would give me a go. The next day, I arrived on the station with all my worldly possessions, my clothes, my tent and a rifle.

Elsey Station was about 5334 square kilometres in area and had the capacity to run about 20,000 head of cattle. As I understood it, the station was named after the Elsey Creek that ran through it, which in turn was named after Dr Elsey, a surgeon who had travelled with the Augustus Charles Gregory expedition, from Victoria River to Queensland, via the Roper River.

I arrived just after the Australian movie We of the Never Never was filmed there. It was directed by Igor Auzins, and had been nominated for five AFI awards and it earned one award for the best cinematography. I asked why the stockyard's fence was so low, as I'd never seen such low fences before. The staff told me they weren't for regular use but had been purpose-built for the movie, so they could get better shots.

---

1 * Ringers are stockmen in the Top End who are only employed for the dry season

Out the back of the homestead was a bunkhouse, which was basically just a row of rooms, each of them 3 x 3 metres square with a mattress on the floor. I dropped my gear in my room and the boss said, "You and a couple of the Aboriginal stockmen should go out and get a killer", which meant we were to get a steer, shoot it and break it up for food for the station, so off we went.

Four hours later, the station cook whipped up a great meal and I fell into bed. In the morning, I woke up and was instantly aware of how sore my feet were. The next night I discovered the cause. I was awoken in the night by something having a good old gnaw at my feet. It turned out to be bloody cockroaches! I didn't sleep another night out there without socks on my feet.

The days were long and hard on Elsey. I drove the bull catcher, a four-wheel drive with a bull bar that could knock over large cattle. It was also tough enough to withstand the ant mounds, which were strong as stone and often more than six-feet high and half a car's width across.

Two Aboriginal guys and I worked like Trojans banging in tar-covered star pickets for the never-ending fencing, using a piece of pipe with a sledgehammer head welded onto it. It was bloody hot work, and the job got even tougher as the temperature increased. One day as I continually wiped sweat from my forehead, I didn't realise that I was actually putting tar on my face. The soaring temperature began to melt the tar onto my face and it burnt badly. When I realised what was happening, I dove straight into a water tank until the tar cooled and I could pull it away. My face peeled after that and it felt as if I had second-degree burns.

While the work on the station was hard and tiring, there were a few upsides. The Northern Territory is known for the elusiveness of the barramundi, but after the wet season on Elsey Station, they were easy to catch.

Once the heavy rains subsided, the fish would be trapped in rock pools and fair game for whoever was hungry—and freshly cooked barra is one of the best meals around. The thermal pools at Mataranka Springs were another highlight of living on the station and a real treat for the body after a long, hard week of work.

Chapter 7

Lucky in love

I'd been on the station for a couple of months when I got word that my car had been repaired. I'd enjoyed my time at Elsey, but it was time to travel the 54-hour bus journey, from Darwin to Brisbane, and then the four hours to Goondiwindi, to collect my trusty Ford Cortina.

When I arrived back in Brisbane, I stayed with Mum, who had a new house in Carina. She had converted the garage into a man cave for me, so I had my own space. The Commonwealth Games were on and Brisbane was buzzing with athletes and spectators from all over the world. There were parties all over the city and people revelled in the exciting atmosphere the Games had brought.

I began working at Downey Finlay's as a storeman/driver, for a great bloke called Peter Finlay, who really looked after us. Every Friday arvo he'd throw me the keys to his Mercedes Benz and say "pop down to the pub and grab a carton of beer for you and the boys"—great boss!

While I had been away, Mum had taken up with a bloke called Tony, an American ex-navy man. It wasn't long before we clashed and I realised I couldn't live at mum's any longer. A mate from rugby, Tommy Seamon, said I was welcome to have the spare room at his flat, so I moved out of mum's and went on to have a ball, working, training and partying with Tommy.

In the meantime, Dad had moved back to Australia with Cherrie. At first, they lived in Dad's Queenslander in Carina, but then they moved to Inala to be closer to the convenience store they had purchased, and which happened to be in the same suburb as Tommy's relatives.

Tommy's folks were fabulous people; they welcomed me into their home as if I was one of the family. One night I was invited over for a family hāngi, where I was one of the only two white people out of about 200 Islanders for the feast. They cooked six whole pigs, over an open coal fire, and different varieties of fish and vegetables were cooking away in two other pits. In addition to the pits, there were all kinds of fruit, some of which I'd never seen before. It was by far the biggest feast I'd ever seen. I stood by the pits for hours with my Tongan friends, turning the pigs and putting butter on them. It was a brilliant night—great food, great people and a lot of laughs.

By the end of 1983, Tommy had met a woman and three was becoming a crowd. So good old Dad said I could move into the Queenslander that he still owned in Carina, which had been sitting empty since he moved to Inala. The deal was that I had to pay the power bills, the rates, and maintain the garden—all two and a half acres of huge macadamia nut trees and lawn. I jumped at it! How many 21-year-olds get the chance to live in a stunning Queenslander on a block of land, by themselves?

It was a fabulous place, quiet and central to work.

Then, in March 1984, while I still working for Downey's, I laid eyes on my beautiful future bride and soul mate, Deb, for the first time. She was only eleven months older than me, but years wiser. I was instantly captivated by her wit and her smile. In many ways, I thought Deb was too good for me; she was perfect in every way.

Every time I went to Deb's work to pick up stock for delivery, I would try to catch a glimpse of her, lingering just a little to stay with her. Her laugh and the twinkle in her eyes gave her mischievous character away. It wasn't long before she stole my heart and I plucked up the courage to ask her out on our first date.

I was as nervous as hell as I drove out to where she lived with her parents. It was just ten minutes from me in Carina, but the drive felt like an hour—I couldn't wait to get there. I drove to her house in my Bedford van, which I'd bought after the death of my Cortina, and which was kitted out like a camper in the back. I'll admit I was shaking a bit, as I got out of the van to meet Terry and Jan, Deb's parents, who were waiting out the front to greet me. We had a chat and my nerves settled, before I whisked their daughter away for an exciting date at the drive-in.

Deb looked fantastic that day. She was wearing blue jeans with a hot pink T-shirt and white sneakers. I was pulling away from her driveway when the mud flap caught on the tyre. I didn't even think, before asking Deb if she wouldn't mind pulling it out so we could move. Without a second's hesitation, she got straight onto it, and I remember thinking to myself, 'What a girl!' A great icebreaker that still makes us smile today.

We didn't get to see much of *The Rocky Horror Picture Show*, because we spent the evening talking about anything and everything. Being with Deb was easy; from the beginning, it felt like I was home in her presence.

Deb's fabulous sense of humour has kept me smiling for over 34 years. On that first date, she told me she and her work mate, Lenny, had a bet going to see which of them would date me first. I said I was bloody glad Deb won, since Lenny was a gay man in his early forties!

From then on, we became inseparable—best friends and lovers. We had so much in common. We had even attended the same high school, which surprised us, as we had never seen each other on campus.

When I first met Deb, I was a bit of a wild boy. Settling down, getting married and having kids was the furthest thing from my mind, but after that first date, I knew Deb was the one for me. I felt as if I had known her for a thousand years and wanted a thousand more with her.

Twelve months after our first date, I popped the question. Deb had been really unwell and was staying at my place. I looked at her lying in bed, helpless and sick as a dog and I just melted. I knelt beside her in the traditional fashion and asked her to marry me. Thankfully, she said yes!

Chapter 8

Digging for gold

After Deb's recovery, she got busy with the wedding arrangements, while Dad and I finalised the arrangements for a gold mining trip to Innisfail that we had been planning for a few months, along with my footy mate Dave McKean.

I resigned from my job at Downey Finlay's and made arrangements for my grandmother, Gran Fuller, to come from Mt Morgan to keep Deb company, while I was away. Gran was a wonderful person, an ice-cream-loving treasure, who was easy-going and happy to help out. With the plans at home all sorted and Deb happy, we were on our way.

We set off with high expectations of striking it rich. The area the mine was in had produced large quantities of gold in the past 100 years. A nearby mine had a seam of quartz that was over two metres wide and had been delivering high returns. Unfortunately, the same mine became unviable, because as the miners got deeper into the earth, water started to seep into the mine, turning it into a huge waterhole.

On the way from Brisbane to Innisfail, we stopped at Rockhampton overnight to visit family, before setting off early the next morning, to drive all the rest of way to our destination. At about 3am we stopped for half an hour on a mountain range to look at the sky, which was full of stars—truly a spectacular sight. Then, we continued on to the town of Innisfail and camped beside the Johnstone River.

We got some sleep, before heading over to Mundoo, just outside of Innisfail, to meet a man by the name of Fred Smith and his partner, from whom Dad had bought the mining lease, some 50km from Mundoo.

We lived in an old caravan that Fred and his partner had towed into the bush years beforehand, to live in while they fossicked themselves. It was very basic, but it kept the rain off us! There was also a 'lean to', so there was plenty of room to rest when we weren't working the mine.

Dad was no stranger to mining. He had worked this same mine when I was about eleven years old, so he knew it intimately and he had everything we needed to make a good go of it, including a backhoe. Our days consisted of getting up at daylight, making brekky and then hooking into it for the day. We made a good start and found traces of gold in just the first two days.

I loved being out there, and as remote as we were, there was always something going on. One night Dave and I were walking up the 2km trail, when we heard a funny noise that sounded like a thump, thump, thump, and it was getting louder and louder. The only weapon we had was a torch that Dave was carrying, so I looked around for the biggest stick I could find in case it was a feral pig or something that was going to come at us.

We were both getting pretty worried, when suddenly a huge cassowary came walking out of the scrub. He barely gave us a once over before continuing his stroll into the bush.

Every five days or so, we'd go into the little town of Milla Milla to get the basic supplies, of milk and bread, etc.

We didn't see many people at the mine, so trips into town were also a good excuse to have a bit of a yak to the locals, and I would steal some time to ring Deb. It was the highlight of my week; I missed her greatly even though she wrote me a letter every day.

One morning while driving back to the mine, Dad came across the only police officer in the whole town, who issued him a speeding ticket. Dad was adamant he wasn't speeding but the cop didn't want to hear about it. Dad had a hard time letting it go; it rubbed him the wrong way and he was very dark about it. A few weeks later, karma played its part.

Dad, Dave and I were walking from the mine to the car, when a copper jumped out from behind a tree and put a gun to my head. I almost shat myself! Within seconds, there were coppers everywhere with handguns and rifles all pointed at us! They were fully kitted out for a raid.

It turns out that an old prospector had seen the two-and-a-half-inch water pipe, which channelled water down to our mine and crushing plant for a distance of about 2 km. He had incorrectly guessed we were growing marijuana in the bush. I think the coppers thought they were about to uncover a major drug's operation—they were as surprised to find we were only gold miners, as we were seeing them with their guns pointing at us.

An hour or so of being interviewed, and having guns pointed at us, did nothing to improve Dad's opinion of the police. So, when the coppers asked Dad if he could give them a lift back to their cars, he asked, "How did you get in here in the first place?" They said they had walked the 10 km from their parking spot. Dad saw his chance for revenge and replied, "Well enjoy your walk!" We jumped into our car and left them to their 10 km hike. I think Dad felt he had gotten even for the speeding ticket.

After three months of digging for gold, we pulled up stumps. I got some of my gold made into a 22-carat ring with the Dickson family crest on it, and the remainder I had made into a piece of jewellery for Deb. Dave went back to Brisbane to play football and got a job working with his brother. Dad got stuck back into his business at Inala, and I helped Deb with the wedding preparations.

Chapter 9

Vows for life

I married my beautiful wife on a clear, sunny day, on January the 18th 1986. All our family and friends were there, with the exception of my mum. She was living in WA with Tony, who wouldn't let her come to our wedding—I was gutted, as was Mum. I married my soul mate in a moving ceremony, with my best man, Dave Kells, and groomsman, Brett McGuinness, by my side. We left the reception in a streamer-strewn, lipstick-painted van with cans trailing behind us, and blazed into a bright future together.

We were so excited to be beginning life as a married couple. I turned to Deb beaming and said, 'Where are we staying?' She looked at me in disbelief, 'That was your job, to book the night!' Married for less than twelve hours and I had already messed up! We drove back to the Queenslander and I called the Park Royal Hotel. Thankfully, their honeymoon suite was available, so a few minutes later we were on our way.

We arrived in our van still covered in all the paraphernalia, and I carried my stunning new bride over the threshold.

The suite was something special, decked out with chilled champagne, chocolates, white bathrobes, slippers and everything we needed for a lovely night.

We spent our honeymoon in Marcoola on the Sunshine Coast. We ate, drank, went to the beach, swam, sun-baked and kicked back. It was perfect apart from the day we fell asleep on the beach and woke up red raw with sunburn—we couldn't move for days, even our eyelids were burned! Lesson learnt there, we never napped on the beach again.

February 1986, and I was back looking for work and doing all sort of jobs, including driving a dodgy Pantech truck for a waterbed company. That truck was a shocker! On my first day, I pulled up to a customer's house and pulled on the hand brake. I had only just climbed out of the vehicle, when it started rolling backwards down the street, right towards the oncoming traffic! I raced after it, dove through the window with my legs hanging out, as frantically reached down to press the brake pedal. I narrowly avoided a bloody disaster! It was one near miss too many for me. The owners couldn't get their head around how dangerous the truck was, so I quit and left them with their heap of crap, hoping it got an early burial before it injured someone.

Fortunately, there was plenty of work around and the next day I began working on the Gateway Arterial Road for Fitzgerald. The hourly rate wasn't fantastic, but

I could do a lot of hours plus weekends, to bring the income up and it was a fabulous opportunity to get my foot into the building industry.

I started at 6:30am and finished about 5pm, and I did a bit of everything from general labouring to driving dump trucks, rollers, backhoes and excavators. One day a section of road needed to be finished, but it had been pouring all day.

The boss got a helicopter to hover over the road, to dry it out, so the bitumen could be laid. Always had a solution that fella!

To bring in more income, I knocked off from Fitzgerald and headed into town three nights a week, to vacuum the offices in the T&G building. On Sunday evenings, I packed fruit and vegetables at the Rocklea Markets. For $100, I worked from 5pm to 5am, before heading straight to work at Fitzgerald at 6:30am, without any sleep. You wouldn't be allowed to do that these days, with all the workplace protocols, but in those days it was just what you did if you wanted to get ahead.

We were working our butts off to save for a car and a house, as were most young couples. Deb was also working full time after which she came home to cook, clean and turn the Queenslander into a beautiful home for us. Having a country background, our work ethic was strong. We just did what we had to do, to achieve the things we wanted and we did it until we had enough in the kitty for me to quit the vacuuming job, and then, eventually, the markets too.

In the middle of 1986, Dad called and asked if I'd come and have a look at a business with him at Tingalpa. With his successful background in caravan parks, he was keen to source another one. The owner, Mrs Davies, had called him to let him know the Nestle Inn Caravan Park was up for sale and she thought that Dad should look at it, because it had good potential for growth.

Dad's plan was to keep the shop at Inala and buy the caravan park, with Deb and me as partners, and managing it together with him and Cherrie. It was an enormous financial commitment for Deb and me, but Mrs Davies was right, there was immense opportunity and Dad and I had the experience to make it work. After a lot of discussion, we signed on the dotted line and Deb and I moved from the Queenslander into the main house on the park grounds and got straight into the job of cleaning it up.

At first, it was a real juggle. Deb had given her employer one month's notice, so she was getting up with me at 4am, to clean the park before racing off to her full-time job. Then it was straight home, to work until late in the park before doing it all again the next day.

As time went on, we got busier and busier. However, we still got up at 4am to clean the toilet blocks, and then Deb would open the office at 6am while I did the garbage pickup with the staff. The day would flow on from there, with a stream of visitors in and out and things to be done.

We knew we were up against it buying the park, but we loved working there together and enjoyed the experience immensely.

Chapter 10

The time of mince and sausages

In 1987, just two days before Deb's 26th birthday, our first son, Christian, came into the world. I was one of the first fathers whom the hospital allowed to be present at the birth of their child and I don't mind saying the experience brought me to tears. Deb said that Christian looked like a girl, he was that pretty, and she was right!

While Deb was still in the hospital, recuperating after having Christian, I was busy at home ripping the bathroom apart to put in a bath to surprise Deb, as there was no proper bath for her or the baby. I worked every spare minute, so I could have it finished before they arrived home.

All was going well, until Deb called to say she was ready to come home a day early. With the bathroom not quite finished, I panicked and suggested she stay there another day—just in case. Well, that didn't go down well and she totally lost it, "Why? Don't you love me anymore?" I hadn't expected that reaction, so I got straight in the car, left the bathroom as it was, and went to collect my newborn son and beautiful wife.

On the way home, I explained to her what I'd been up to and why I had suggested she stay an extra day. Suffice to say I was back in her good books.

Life at the park didn't slow because we had a newborn to look after. Life just got more hectic and then Dad was diagnosed with diabetes. He was determined to keep doing what he always had done and not to let his diabetes slow him down. He had energy and his drive motivated all of us.

We had a great staff on board at the park, helping with the operational side and ensuring it ran smoothly. Ralph, Cherrie's brother, emigrated from the Philippines and joined the staff as well—he was a good bloke, and a hard worker who showed wonderful versatility, lending his hand to just about anything, including saving my son's life.

Christian had been really sick with the flu and he stopped breathing. Deb and Ralph were the only ones on the park grounds and Deb was terrified, but Ralph quickly jumped into action, sucking the blockage from Christian's nose to clear his airway. I'll be forever grateful to Ralph for doing what he did.

A year later, our family was complete with the arrival of our second son. Zeik was born beautiful and healthy, less than 20 months after Christian's birth.

Expo 88 was an incredibly busy time as tourists flocked to Brisbane from all over the world. Even though the park was at peak capacity, Deb and I took a rare day off to visit the wonderful event.

There were displays from all over the world and it was a sight to see the pavilions, art works and entertainment. The event, which was themed 'The Age of Technology', averaged 100,000 visitors per day and the atmosphere was incredible.

As the park continued to grow, we sought and received approval to extend it by a further 100 sites. We had no sewage infrastructure for that area, which meant we would have to build our own 2 km line, from the sewage main to the site. It took us three days of blood, sweat and almost some tears as we slogged it out digging the long ditch. I drove the backhoe to do some of the heavier work and we used a ditch witch trencher to dig through to the mains' sewer. Once that was done, the rest was easier—we laid the sewer line, put the sand in over the top of it, and filled it in with dirt. It was a champion effort by everyone.

Once the line was in, we began clearing the area where the new sites would go—up the back of the property, nestled amongst the native Australian scrub trees. We cleared the trees and scrub selectively, to keep as much natural vegetation as possible and to retain the beauty of the area, before building roads and a pump station. They say that each job you have in life prepares you for something in the future. I can definitely agree with that because the whole project would have cost us a bomb if I had not had the skills I'd developed working for Fitzgerald and Dad over the years.

The 100 new sites meant a sharp increase in guests and we were kept on our toes, but it was worth it, the business boomed. We had good staff, good guests and a great little lifestyle—we were in a really good place and were having a ball designing and implementing special activities to bring smiles to our visitors' faces.

The majority of our sites were occupied by permanent residents. Our visitors were families or grey nomads, travelling around and happy to be on holidays, and a pleasure to have staying with us.

There were also couples that came in on weekend camping adventures and the odd single short-stayer.

One guy, who came in short-term, was a very sad story. He arrived at the park having just broken up with his wife and was clearly down on his luck, with nowhere else to go. He had only been there a few days, when a resident came into the office from the back of the park saying there was a bloke in a car, who kept blowing his car horn. I immediately went up there and was shocked to find the poor man inside his car passed out and slumped over the wheel. Looking through the window, I saw he had hooked a pipe from the exhaust to gas himself.

I frantically tried all the doors, which were locked before I smashed the window to unlock the door and drag him out. I performed mouth-to-mouth and CPR to no avail. It was bloody terrible to see this fit, healthy young man end his life like that. All I could think of was he was someone's dad, someone's brother, someone's best friend, and he was gone. So incredibly sad!

My days at the park were spent doing the outside work: filling gas bottles, cleaning toilets, doing the rubbish run and loading coal for the boilers (the cheapest way to get hot water) into the shed. I sold ice at the entrance to the park to boost the income, and renovated some old railway camp wagons that we rented out. These were a real hit with families as they slept six in the berths. There was always a lot to do to keep me busy.

Deb ran the office, taking rent money, manned the shop and cleaned the caravans when they became vacant, while working at being a mum to two busy little boys.

Christian basically grew up on the office floor and could answer the phone by the time he was four years old. His telephone skills came in very handy, when he had to call 000 to save Deb's life.

She went into anaphylactic shock after taking an antibiotic that had sulphur in it, which we discovered she was allergic to. I gave Deb mouth-to-mouth, while Christian called an ambulance.

While Dad continued to work the shop at Inala, Cherrie took care of the books for both businesses. We had been kicking along like this for about five years when Cherrie took off with a young bloke from the caravan park, and we discovered she had also been misusing funds. We were turning over a healthy $13,000 a week and should have been streets ahead, but Cherrie hadn't paid a single bill for months. We called it 'the time of mince and sausages' because that's all we could afford to eat after paying ourselves $200 a week.

After Cherrie left, I took over the finances and called every creditor we had, to explain the situation to them. Deb and I had purchased a house at Birkdale for $64,000 about eighteen months earlier, so we put it up for sale and made about $30,000 profit. This helped pay off a great deal of the overdue debt and I brokered a payment plan for the rest of it. Dad sold the shop at Inala and life went on as we focused on rebuilding the business.

In 1991, Mum returned to Brisbane, after divorcing Tony. It was wonderful to have her back in our lives and to watch her bonding with her grandsons. She also rekindled her relationship with Dad and before long they were back together, which made us all very happy. Mum and Dad worked the park with us, along with Sandra's husband Colin.

However, the legacy of Cherrie's actions had placed a tremendous toll on the family. We busted our butts to get back into the black and the pressure wore us down physically and emotionally. We made a huge dent in it, but we were all exhausted and began to burn out. Deb and I were at capacity, raising the boys and working all the time, and one evening we sat down, looked at each other and said it was enough. We needed something better for our family and we wanted to spend more time with our sons.

Dad wasn't overly happy when I told him that Deb and I wanted to sell up and move on, but he understood—we were a young family and had put in the miles with the business. We wanted to keep things simple and give the boys our time and an adventure here and there, so we decided to sell the caravan park.

After leaving the park, we did a bit of this and that in Brisbane, including owning a shoe repair shop. We bought two opal mine leases in the sheep yards near Lightning Ridge and every school holidays for the next two years we would headed south-west for mining adventures. The boys loved it! There were no phones, TV or people—just us, the bush, the campfire and the underground mine. We made a lot of great memories on those trips and it gave us all a chance to have a bush change from the city.

Chapter 11

Our forever home

Mum and Dad headed north and bought a lovely lodge in the hinterland town of Montville. Dad called me about five months after they had moved to say there was a property for sale next door and I should take a look—he thought it would be fantastic for us. He was right! We instantly fell in love, bought it, packed up our Brisbane life and moved to the Sunshine Coast and a better life.

Montville is the quintessential hinterland village. It is built on the range amongst lush green paddocks and dotted with cottages and boutique shops. This setting gave me the idea for my next venture—a horse-drawn carriage business.

As well as driving tourists around, we did plenty of weddings—it was definitely a change! It was peaceful driving the two ex-trotters, listening to the sound of their hooves in the foggy early morning streets, or  the crisp romantic evenings with lovers cuddled up behind me in the carriage. Dad would often come along for the ride, just spending time with me and shooting the breeze. He had begun to slow down and although I didn't know it, he was already getting pretty crook.

In May 1996, we sold our house to finance the purchase of 64 magical acres further up the road in Montville. We bought an old Queenslander and transported it from Brisbane to our new property. I can vividly remember it arriving, in two sections on separate trucks. Getting the house up the steep embankment to its final resting position, on the knoll of our property, was a monumental task, but it was well worth it for the spectacular views of the Sunshine Coast.

We still laugh today at the length of time it took to have the new roof installed. The roofers would be on top of the house and could see the waves at the beach, so off they'd go, "Surfs up!" I'm sure they had a set of binoculars in their toolbox. But hey, could you blame them! They were young and you only live once.

It took us twelve months to finish the renovation, but once it was done, it looked incredible. Our new home boasted the best views in Montville, and we often reflected on just how lucky we were to live there.

Our boys, Christian and Zeik, were doing well in school. Deb helped out in the tuck shop and sold her craft works in some of the boutique shops in town. We sold the horse carriage business and I was still working at the motel and had joined the rural fire brigade. It was a fantastic community with great people that we loved being part of.

As with everything in life, the good often comes with the bad. By 1997, Dad's health had taken a turn for the worse. He lost his sight, had a toe cut off and then a leg. The diabetes had taken hold and he was losing the battle. We were all devastated when he passed away on February the 25th. He was my hero and he was gone. He had taught and given me so much more than he'll ever know. He really did shape the man I am, and I still miss him greatly.

By the end of the 1990s, the boys were well into their teens and had discovered a love of the beach and skateboarding. We had gotten into the habit of making the forty-minute trek down the mountain every other day, so the boys could catch up with their mates or play sport. The fuel was costing a bomb and we were going through brake pads like there was no tomorrow, I kid you not!

Around the same time, Deb got really sick with whooping cough and then began to get asthma. We didn't realise it but the pollutants from the coast were rising up into the hinterland, which is what was bringing her asthma on. Once we realised this, we understood it would never get better if we stayed where we were, so we decided to sell our magnificent Queenslander and head closer to the beach.

Within a couple of months, we had a buyer, who told us their dream was to start a vineyard and winery on the property. To our surprise, they said they were looking for partners and asked us if we'd be interested. Deb and I thought it sounded like a fabulous investment, so we stayed in Montville for a further six months investing a significant amount of money and time to help get the business off the ground.

We planted vines, put up posts and strainer wire to support the grapes, set up the underground watering system and basically got the place ship-shape before moving down to the coast and leaving them to run it with a manager in place.

In April 1999, we moved into what we call our 'forever home'. It was truly our best move yet. We had searched high and low to find a home that would suit our needs. Our boys needed room to run and play, and Deb and I are both keen gardeners and love making a house a home with our own style of renovation.

It was a few weeks before we found our piece of paradise in Mons, on the fringe of Buderim. It consisted of two-and-a-half acres with a creek running through the back portion of the property, about 420 feet above sea level. It was close to schools, shops, the beach, and only one hour from Brisbane Airport—it couldn't be better than that.

The house was solidly built but needed some of Deb's creativity and TLC. The gardens were also in need of some love and care, as the previous owners had become unwell and couldn't keep up with the workload. They had created the beginnings of a magnificent garden that we have enhanced over the twenty-one years we've called the property home.

All our hard work in the garden was rewarded, when local garden club asked us if we would open our garden to the public for a fundraiser over a full weekend. We were thrilled to have been asked, they were a wonderful group of people. We worked on it for months to get everything up to scratch for that one weekend and it looked fantastic. Over the course of the weekend, thousands of people strolled through our garden and enjoyed what we experience every day. To this day, being part of the Buderim Garden Festival is a memory both Deb and I cherish.

Chapter 12

Throwing my hat into the ring

Going from working for myself to working for the community and, ultimately, into politics wasn't a huge leap. I had always had a passion for helping people, a belief in fair play and a 'can do' solution-focused attitude.

Gradually, reading the local paper, watching the local news and listening to the community's ever-increasing frustration over council fees, charges and lack of transparency began to drive me mad. I thought about my grandfather's role as a councillor, for 32 years, and Dad's term as a councillor in Mount Morgan, before we moved to Brisbane. I tossed it over a bit, before reaching a turning point, after we experienced the frustration of bureaucracy for ourselves.

In 1997, we applied to sub-divide our Montville property into two lots. The local councillor at the time said to us, "If you donate the creek that runs through your property and the land on either side of it to council, then you won't have any problems getting your subdivision".

This heavy handedness was just one of a number of issues I'd been discussing with Sunshine Coast residents, various community groups, and even within the Rural Fire Brigade. One common concern for many people was that the coastal strip got all the funding and other areas were left behind. I couldn't argue with them because it was true.

The drive from Montville to the coast was a perfect example of the 'us and them' dichotomy, as the community put it. Driving down Razorback Road was dusty, dangerous and it was in need of sealing.

Moreover, many services that coastal residents took for granted were not available in the hinterland—sewage, public transport, town water, etc. The list just grew and grew.

However, although the coastal areas did fair better than the hinterland, there were still parts of the coast that had to deal with unsealed roads. The community believed the council was not focusing on the community's priorities. I also listened to many discussions about planning—what the Sunshine Coast would look like in twenty years' time. We knew this planning was important and would affect everyone—and the local government and the elected councillors would be making decisions regarding growth and planning for our futures.

One day, Deb finally got tired of listening to me banging on about how our politicians were letting us down and raving about the councillor. She said, "Well stop talking about it and do something about it! You're a local; maybe you could take on the role of our community champion."

With Deb's full support and a fire in my belly, I made my decision to run for council. I was committed to fixing the issues, through strong leadership and by putting people first. I knew how I felt and what was important to me; now it was time to get out there and find out what my community was thinking, and what they wanted.

I quickly realised that the key to political success is knocking on doors, and knock I did, on every door *twice* in an eighteen-month period.

Even though I went through several pairs of shoes, it was the best thing I could have done, because it was the only way to discover what was on people's minds. I mostly found common themes existed about what the issues were, what was going well and what needed fixing.

A number of the houses I approached, within the division, had Kiwis living in them, who were disappointed they couldn't vote. I regularly heard people say, "We are not registered voters so our opinion doesn't count" or, "We'd like to vote, but we can't." I always said to them, "Your opinion is just as important as anyone else's—you know what's happening in your neighbourhood, your kids go to the local school. I'd like to know what you think needs fixing". In some ways, it was more valuable feedback than I received generally. Because they couldn't vote, they were open and forthcoming with their thoughts and ideas. It was just as important to me as it was to them.

In addition to knocking on doors, I attended every public meeting I could, to learn as much as possible about what was going on in my community. I wanted to know what issues were important and what the potential solutions were, so I could stand up and speak about them confidently, and find the right people to make the changes possible.

With my research done and a solid understanding of what my community wanted, I turned up at the council chambers, paid my fee and was nominated to run for council. My campaign policies included: not voting against the wishes of my constituents; stopping the introduction of drinking treated sewage water; building new footpaths; sealing dirt roads and not having my strings pulled by others who might have had conflicts of interest.

My wife, family and friends rallied around me and were incredible supporters, as were many members of our community. There was no shortage of help as we coordinated my campaign, handed out 'how to vote' cards, placed signage up and talked with the media.

Election day was March the 25th 2000, and I crossed my fingers as we turned out in force at the booths to convey my primary election points and gain support. It was a huge day for us all. As the polling booths closed, Deb and I went to the council chambers to watch the ballot being counted. Upon arrival, I was 54 votes behind—by the time the vote had been completely counted, I had won by a clear majority. We were so excited about what the future held for our community, now I could make a real difference!

I went outside to have a quiet moment and smoked the last cigarette I ever smoked. I counted my lucky stars on how blessed I was to have such fantastic people around me, and I reflected on all their hard work, and the campaign. I sent silent thanks to every single person, who had helped get me elected, especially those who voted for me. I stubbed out the cigarette and got down to business.

My first council meeting was held in the Fred Murray Building in Nambour, an impressive building, which was home to the council chambers. The councillors seemed to fall into two distinctive groups: those who were for development and those who didn't believe in development at any cost. I didn't fall into either group; for me it was about fair play, smart development, and making sure the ratepayers were well represented.

Chapter 13

A promise made is a promise kept

I was now the councillor for Division 8, covering the areas of Sippy Downs, Buderim, Mons and Forest Glen on the Sunshine Coast.

Each division has different boundaries; some are larger than others are, but they all comprise a similar number of people. Division 8 was small in land area, but had a very high population. My portfolio included being a member of the Maroochy-Caloundra Water Board and a member of the Caravan Park Advisory Board, which—given my background—I really enjoyed.

Being on the Water Board enabled me to keep one of my election promises, to stop the introduction of treated sewage water as drinking water, popularly known as recycled water. Instead, we drew upon the Baroon Pocket Dam to supply water to the Maroochy and Caloundra Shire Council areas, using an advanced water treatment called ozonation. This involved injecting ozone into water that was particularly high in pathogens, thereby removing the bacteria and viruses. The water was then put through one of eight special filters, lined with biologically activated carbon (BAC). It was the best and cheapest outcome and produced the best quality water in the state.

I soon discovered the council was on the brink of real financial trouble and this, along with many important issues had been hidden from the community, which I thought was wrong.

We were spending he community's dollars and they had a right to know they weren't being managed properly.

I felt an open conversation was important and although there were councillors who disagreed, I wasn't about to keep quiet. I made some statements to the media that ended up on the front page of the local newspaper—the Sunshine Coast Daily. I believed transparency concerning these types of issues were essential if things were to change for the better, however the ruling block in council didn't like it.

As we were sitting in the meeting room, with the full council and all the managers, I was asked why I had made the statement public. I said, "Because the council is being poorly run and something needs to change to get it back in the black". The twenty-five people in the room were glued to their seats, but the CEO took my comment personally. He stormed across the room, towards me in a complete rage.

Undeterred by his bullying, I stood up and said, "Don't try something that I may have to finish". Well, that did it! He launched himself at me, as two councillors jumped up and grabbed hold of him. I stood my ground and that was my baptism into local government. To his credit, he later apologised for his blow up.

The Caravan Park Advisory Board allowed me to use the skills I'd acquired working in Dad's caravan park and owning my own. We introduced onsite cabins, in addition to the caravans we had; we upped the quality of accommodation and the income. Sunshine Coast Caravan Park was owned by the people of the coast and had so much to offer—I felt the role was made for me.

The council received a number of complaints about the lake system. It was overgrown with weeds and full of rubbish. I got to work cleaning up and rejuvenating the lakes in Chancellor Park that I had inherited from a planning environment court decision.

At the end of the first phase, the lakes looked a million dollars and the neighbourhood felt proud that the community had invested themselves into it. The current divisional councillor, my son Christian, completed the remainder of the lake system.

The planning and remodelling process of Forest Glen began at my instigation. I had sewerage connected to the area and took the opportunity to put plans in place to fix the traffic problems that had been giving the community a huge headache. I brought all the landholders together in one room, at the Fred Murray building, and brokered a deal for them to contribute to the cost of the sewerage installation, and to start the planning process that would bring Forest Glen to life. It would mean jobs, a new road network and a renewal of the area. I was pleased with the progress I was making in such a short time.

I couldn't just rest on my laurels though. There was still a lot to do on my pre-election list. Next up was the local dog owners' wish for somewhere in Buderim to take their furry friends to run, exercise and socialise. I built the first dedicated dog park on the Sunshine Coast, with the help of Lynn Moss, a local community advocate, who had been asking council to come up with a plan for six months.

In fact, Buderim's dog park was so successful that other parks have been built since. To this day, I enjoy hearing stories about like-minded people meeting at dog parks. My favourite is about the couple who met there while exercising their dogs and who went on to get married! I'm sure there will be more stories to come in the future.

Another major community issue was that the council was always pushing for smaller blocks of land, to squeeze in more dwellings. They continued to try to convince me of the economy of scale. Many of those in property development also wanted more blocks per hectare, but it wasn't what the people wanted so I pushed back, fighting hard against smaller housing blocks across the entire Maroochy Shire.

In my electorate of Buderim there was a development called Rainforest Sanctuary, where the consultants and the council staff wanted to develop 400-metre-square blocks. This went against what I was fighting for, so I rang the developer, Wayne Rex, who was the head of Stockland. He and I sat down and discussed the matter, and we agreed that the minimum block size would be 700m². He was happy, the community was happy, and everyone came out a winner.

Chapter 14

Creative councillor

In my early days of local government, I loved thinking outside of the box to find solutions to the issues that the community faced. They were wide ranging, for example, how to establish more employment for school leavers and the people moving into the area, as well as creating prospects for career development, such as moving forward on the approval and construction of the Homemaker Centre in Maroochydore.

As each area grew, new challenges emerged that needed attention and alternative strategies, which would benefit the local community and make life easier. I have to say, I got lucky with my community. Not only were the residents proactive and passionately invested in their area but they were also forthcoming about what they needed and wanted, which was wonderful for me as their representative.

Every other day I met another amazing individual, businessperson or community group who were working hard for something they believed in. They were an endless source of inspiration for me and the motivation to work even harder to help get them what they needed.

Some had fought against all the odds, but still hadn't had the hand-up they desperately needed—not only for their cause but also for their spirit. There were always worthy causes that required help, from charities to sporting clubs.

I was able to go into council and bat for some of the groups, while I had to help other with my annual divisional allocated funds, which I normally used to build things such as children's playgrounds.

One sporting group that reached out for assistance was the Buderim Wanderers Football Club, whose aim was to get more young people involved in sport. They were a great group of people, who operated like one big happy family, rolling their sleeves up and pitching in at their regular working bees. The club had been fundraising for ages to get their car park resurfaced. You should have seen it! It was reminiscent of the back roads of the Philippines—full of potholes and rough as guts.

At the time, the council didn't offer much assistance to sporting groups so I took on the project and used some of my divisional allocation to get the car park sealed. It looked fantastic and the club were so over the moon they invited me to be their patron. I joined a long and esteemed list of predecessors including the popular mayors, Eddie Devere and Fred Murray, both of whom had been patrons for twenty years.

With not enough allocated funds to go around, I donated part of my councillor's wage increase to a wonderful charity called Bloomhill, an integrated care and fundraising organisation to help enhance the quality of life for people living with cancer. I believed they needed all the help they could get to help as many people affected by cancer as possible. The work they do is truly amazing; they are a very worthwhile cause.

However, the council did come through on many occasions thankfully, such as when the Sippy Downs Community Association and the local Chancellor State School were in need of a hall that both of them could use. I met with the Sippy Downs Community Association, the school principal and the P&C, to draft a business plan that included an afterschool and vacation care centre, which would create cash flow. We got Education Queensland on board and I put a motion to council to put $125,000 towards construction of the much-needed hall. Council accepted the motion, the hall was constructed and a memorandum of understanding was drawn up to provide for school, P&C and community use. The hall is used for out of school care and it has hosted thousands of school events; including graduations, school discos and parades, as well as local sporting group sign ups and numerous other community events.

One of the councillors, who served at the same time as I did, was Erroll Middlebrook, a passionate man, who also put the community first, for which I admired him. He helped establish the privately owned consortium, Cow Candy, on the Sunshine Coast after the local sugar mill closed in Nambour in 2003, after operating since 1887.

Cow Candy was organised to take up the cane quota that was left behind when the mill closed and it cut sugar cane for livestock consumption, both here and overseas. Erroll loved to help people—he was a farmer, a dozer driver, a mechanic, and a jack-of-all-trades. He and his wife, Dell, were well known for taking in homeless people to stay on their property or to work on it if they needed money. Erroll had a shot at running for mayor in the 2004 election. It was unfortunate he didn't win because he would have served the council and the community well.

Working for council was never boring as there was so much diversity to the job. Joe Natoli and I teamed up to deliver initiatives that would attract more visitors to the Sunshine Coast. We were part of the group who obtained the Australian PGA Championship, in 2002. This wonderful tournament stayed in the region until 2013, when Clive Palmer bought the Hyatt and transformed it into a dinosaur resort—I kid you not! Sadly, the resort has been closed for a number of years now.

In 2004, Joe and I used $5000 from each of our discretionary funds to help fund the sinking of the HMAS Brisbane directly out from Alexandra Headland. We'd never had anything like that before, and our beautiful clear water made it a scuba diver's dream come true. The actual sinking of the ship, a couple of years later attracted local residents in their thousands, who watched from the headland as the ship slowly settled to the ocean floor. In a matter of months, the wreck, which was managed by the ex-HMAS Brisbane Conservation Park, was transformed into an artificial reef and natural habitat for marine life that is fabulous draw card for visiting and local scuba divers.

Not only had I found a career that perfectly suited me but I was also in my element, assisting people with minor and major issues. Being instrumental in helping others is something special and I found it an incredibly rewarding profession.

Chapter 15

Memorable moments

The calibre of events I attended, in my time with the Maroochy Shire Council, was quite astonishing. From taking part in Virgin Airlines' celebrating flying into the Sunshine Coast Airport, by holding promotional events with Richard Branson, Natalie Imbruglia and Marcia Hines, to being part of the Olympic torch relay, I was truly blessed.

Not long after I was elected into council, I had the honour of being selected to carry the Olympic flame down Jones Road in Buderim. I'd actually been selected twice, once as a community representative and once as an AMP member. It was a huge thrill and while I would have happily carried it twice, I didn't think it was fair doing someone else out of the opportunity to carry it.

The moment was made even more memorable, knowing I would be following in my Dad's footsteps, yet again. He had carried the flame, in 1956, in the Marlborough area of Queensland, just north of Rockhampton.

It was three years since Dad had passed, but I felt him with me every step I took as I carried the flame. I ran slowly, savouring every second of it. In one hand, I held the flame and in the other, I carried the medal Dad received when he carried the flame all those years ago. I thought about him and the conversation we'd had before his death about his race. How fortunate that both of us had the privilege of being part of Olympic history.

At the end of my leg of the relay, I met up with runner 046 who stood beside me while I lit their torch with mine. Once you've lit the next flame, you're supposed to extinguish your flame, take the gas cylinder out and discard it, but I kept mine for something that was planned for later on.

My next duty as a councillor was to greet the last runner to arrive at the Nambour Showgrounds. I'll never forget the drive there and neither will my wife. Deb had a Hyundai coupe with a sunroof and I'm not embarrassed to say that I was like a big kid waving the torch out through the sunroof, to everyone as she slowly made her way through the waiting crowd. It was a tonne of fun with lots of smiles all around.

That night, the Maroochy Shire Council hosted a banquet for a foreign delegation at the Twin Waters Resort. After quickly washing and drying the Olympic outfit I'd worn during the run, I put it back on and headed to the function. By the time I arrived, the event had started and the delegation and guests were already seated. Upon my arrival, the event coordinator dimmed the lights and I entered the room carrying the Olympic flame, lit by the gas cylinder that I had kept.

The atmosphere in the room was amazing and I felt like a rock star making my way through the throng of people. The foreign delegates were initially silent, and then they broke out in cheers and applause, excited to see the Olympic torch within arms reach.

I was incredibly lucky to have had such a long time with the torch. It was an immense honour and one I'll treasure forever.

After the Olympic flame was extinguished, it was time to knuckle back down and resume working on my list of the remaining election promises as well as more of the current issues that had cropped up, since I had been elected.

A continually ongoing issue was when a developer tried to strongarm someone and to destroy fragile or important environmental areas. The discrepancy of rights, both within and without the council, never seemed to stop. One particularly massive dispute occurred between two landowners.

One was a local called Peter Wise and the other the father of an Olympian. The dispute was over a swimming pool that had been built over the boundary of Peter Wise's farm. Peter's family had owned the land for over 100 years and he wasn't about to accept someone building on his land and claiming it as their own. Peter invited Cr. Erroll Middlebrook and me over to his house, to inspect the alleged illegal pool and its surrounding structure. After surveying the area, we found it had definitely been built over the boundary and not by a centimetre or so, but by a number of metres.

Peter wanted the councillors to understand that it was *his* land, and no one had the right to build anything on his family property. You couldn't argue with that—he was on point and we were with him 100 percent. I took the information back to a council meeting, where the CEO and council officers had already come to the conclusion that Peter's land should be transferred over to the fellow who had built the pool over the boundary. The court also favoured the encroachment on Mr Wise's family farm, and directed the council to approve the swimming pool and to seal the deal to legitimise the structure.

I for one was not going to sit back and let it happen. A heated debate followed between all involved and I stated that if the court wanted to approve the pool and structure then I didn't want any part of it. It wasn't right taking someone's land for private use. Thankfully, the majority of councillors supported Erroll and I, but the issue went on for eleven years before the pool was eventually removed. Peter ended up writing a book about it called *This Land is My Land!*

Another contentious debate erupted over a multi-storey car park at the popular beachside suburb of Mooloolaba. Didn't we battle over that! The community didn't want a developer to come in and develop council-owned land, in the heart of this picturesque coastal area. Together with a number of councillors, I tried to protect the site from development for years. It became very heated with many protest rallies, newspaper articles and council meetings regarding the project. It finally came down to the public tender process. The council did not go out for the required time, for the tender process, so the whole deal fell over, which was a win for those of us who opposed it.

Sadly, years later when I was out of office, the council sold half the public land to a developer, who has almost finished construction of a multi-storey public car park—it's so disheartening. It looks bloody awful plonked on a block of land one street back from the beach and completely overshadows the whole feel of the area.

Thankfully, I won a lot more of the battles than I lost, and I was proud to have delivered all my election promises. My term in local government was very busy, but I felt as if I hadn't even scratched the surface of doing what I could for our community.

Chapter 16

Dipping my toe into the water

The next election arrived and I was elated to be re-elected. It meant my community was happy with me representing them, with what I had delivered in my previous term. Joe Natoli was elected mayor and I was given my choice of roles (deputy mayor, planning chair, etc.), as my colleagues had given me their majority support. I chose to take on the role of Chairman of Town Planning. It would provide a great challenge for me, but I knew I was ready for it.

Council had about 70 appeals currently before the court system, which I thought was excessive. I spoke to the council CEO, John Knaggs, and said, "How about we get these people in and start solving some of these problems!" And we did. By the time I left that position, there were only 17 appeals left to settle. To me it was about solving issues with common sense, communication, listening and by focusing on solutions. The lawyers had been making a fortune and ratepayers were picking up the tab so working through a good deal of them was a win for everyone—except the lawyers of course!

It was fairly early in my term in local council, when four senators approached me—at different times—to talk me into running for the Queensland Liberal Party (now called the LNP). They were George Brandis, Russell Trood, Brett Mason and Santo Santoro.

I hadn't given it any thought previously, and wasn't overly interested in party politics at the time. I had an armload of projects I was focused on delivering in my electorate, some of which were quite challenging. However, I began to think about how much easier it could be to get them across the line, if there was a bit of state government weight behind them.

I was chatting to Deb about one of my projects, over dinner one night, and threw out the casual line, "I should run for state government, and then it would be a walk in the park getting this through with state funding". I wouldn't say it was a serious conversation, but it soon became one, as we tossed it over and discussed the 'what ifs'.

The entire reason I was in politics was to help my community overcome bureaucratic stupidity. I also wanted to create a fairer system for all, to preserve our environment and to plan for our future. The more Deb and I talked, the more seriously I began to entertain the idea, as it became obvious that being in state government would allow me to achieve more and implement even more in my community.

Discussions over the following weeks led to Deb's asking me straight out, "Do you really want to do this?" We both knew it was a giant risk for us, personally. We were in a great place in all aspects of our life, so why risk it. On the other hand, I had signed up to serve the community and entering state parliament was an additional way to provide that service.

The local MP at the time, Chris Cummins, who served as the Minister for Emergency Services from February 2004 to July 2005 and as the Minister for Small Business, Information Technology Policy and Multicultural Affairs from July 2005 to September 2006, had upset a heap of people, including me. On several occasions, he'd forgotten whom he was working for—the party or the people.

One such occasion involved the parking issue at Chancellor State School, which had been crying out for years to be fixed. I had been pushing for a piece of government owned land to be kept for parents at the school to park on, but Chris wanted it for his own purposes and allowed it to be redeveloped.

This put even more strain on parking and road congestion in the area and removed the opportunity to fix the problem for once and for all.

I came out swinging! He'd completely missed the mark on what the community needed and had made their problems even worse! He retaliated by personally attacking me in parliament; it was game on! It was also the last push I needed in making my decision to go into state government. With Deb's full support, I threw my hat into the ring and embarked on what was to become a fantastic eleven years in state politics.

In 2003, I was nominated for the seat of Kawana for the Liberal Party, but lost the pre-selection to Harry Burnett. Obviously, this was a disappointment for me in more ways than one. Now, I would now have to bide my time and wait until 2006, to have another shot at it. In the meantime, I continued to focus on doing what I could for the community, with the resources that I had, until I was nominated in the next election three years later.

The state elections occurred in September 2006. Fortunately, I won the pre-selection this time and was excited to begin campaigning. It meant a lot to me. I had to win—for my family *and* my community.

Campaigning for state government was different to campaigning for local council elections. Instead of having to design and print my own voting cards and do everything from marketing to walking the pavement, the Liberal Party and its hard-working volunteers in Brisbane ran the entire campaign. They designed and printed the mail outs, signs and advertising. All I needed to do was do what I loved best about campaigning and that was go out knocking on doors and talking to my community. This was complemented by the enormous support of grassroots volunteers, who fundraised, co-ordinated people for pre-poll and election day, set up booths, placed corflutes, and prepared for media engagements and public meet-the-candidate forums.

The campaign was looking absolutely fantastic and I was pleased with how I was looking pre-election, until the Liberal Party decided to have a surprise party change with Bruce Flegg rolling Bob Quinn for leadership. The entire Liberal campaign went to custard with voters getting nervous about the party's stability.

When the voting closed, I was on tenterhooks, waiting at the Headland-Buderim Croquet Club with one hundred or so supporters—including my family and friends—for the numbers to come in. I watched the results unfold on a large television screen and grew quietly confident as the crowd gathered and the numbers came flooding in. When the final tally was made, I'd won the seat of Kawana, against Chris Cummins, the ALP minister, with 49.91% of the primary vote.

It was a sweet win and a great honour and privilege to represent the area I lived in. I was excited and keen to get my teeth into some projects and policies that would make a significant difference for the Sunshine Coast, which always seemed to play second fiddle to Brisbane and the Gold Coast.

Chapter 17

Out of the pot and into the fire

In September 2006, I was officially sworn in as the Liberal member for Kawana and I became a member of Queensland's 52nd Parliament.

In our first meeting as Members of Parliament (MP) for Queensland, there were eight Liberals out of 89 members, under a Peter Beattie-led ALP government. I had to choose which role I would take on. My pick was Shadow Deputy Whip under Ian Rickuss MP, a role that helps organise all the opposition members and ensuring ensures they are in the House to deliver speeches, vote etc. I also was responsible for negotiating with the government Whip on speaking orders.

Taking on this role gave me the opportunity to understand how the parliament worked, as well as who was who, and how to get things done. It was the perfect way for me to become educated in the inner workings of the Parliament. Forming strong new working relationships and communicating effectively with all personnel also paved a great foundation for my first term.

On August the 12th 2008, I stepped from the role of Shadow Whip into the Shadow Minister for Workplace and Job Security's role. I headed out to speak to as many business owners as I could, about any issues they were facing and how we, the LNP Party, could help them succeed, now and in the future.

Two challenges were predominant back then and we needed to get in and do something about them. The first was that crippling electricity costs were negatively affecting businesses and households across the state. The second was the impact of payroll tax. The only way to fix these two problems was to win government and to convince my colleagues that we should change the way the government approached and operated both.

In 2009, the Sunshine Coast was booming, and so the Electoral Commission redistributed the area. My seat of Kawana was pinned as the fastest growing area in terms of population, so they split it in two, creating a new seat of Buderim. At the next election in 2009, I became the member for Buderim, gaining 57.02% of the primary vote.

As the inaugural Member for Buderim, I was sworn in to the 53rd Parliament as Shadow Minister for Energy and Water Utilities. I was re-elected three years later, in 2012, with 62.17% of the primary vote and took on the role of Minister for National Parks, Recreation, Sport and Racing in the Campbell Newman government.

Campbell was the Lord Mayor of the Brisbane City Council, before he threw his hat into state politics and he was a true leader. He had an unwavering desire to bring positive change and he made the hard decisions that others were too afraid to tackle, while running a well-loved local council. His countless achievements in one of Australia's biggest cities put him on the map as a person with a 'can do' attitude.

I'd met him on a Saturday afternoon at a park in Beerburrum, many months before he became leader of the LNP. I wanted to find out if he would ask some of his councillors to run for state government at the next election. We needed good people and he had them in his council. He said he had a different idea. "What do you think of me resigning as Lord Mayor of Brisbane and becoming Leader of the Opposition?" I chuckled, nodding my head and said, "Your idea is better than mine!" He had my full support and confidence and I was delighted when he got in.

The portfolios I had been given suited me well and I enjoyed them immensely. My role allowed me to open up opportunities for ecotourism by changing the Nature Conservation Act, and opening up more national parks for grazing minimised the impact of bushfires and saved animals from starvation.

Within the same portfolio, I was also able to save the green turtles of Raine Island, which was a great achievement. Green turtles were laying their eggs on Raine Island only for them to be inundated with seawater hours later, which killed the unborn turtles. My idea was to raise the height of the island. After negotiations with Greg Hunt, the Federal Environment Minister, we agreed on the solution to save the species from a deteriorating and uninhabitable island, to one that was raised above the inundation level. Survival rates in the trial areas increased from zero to at least 80 percent.

I also opened up camping areas, some of which had been closed by the previous government, to horse riding along the beaches, mountain biking through the parks and forests and rock climbing. One in particular was the Eungella National Park camping area, a beautiful park where you could go for a walk through the rainforest and eucalypts and see all sorts of unusual plants and animals—definitely one place to put on your bucket list.

As a sportsman myself, and the father of boys who really enjoyed playing sports growing up, as well as supporting sport, well-being and activity were other areas I had my eye on. I was aware that the high cost of sport fees made it difficult for some parents to keep their kids in sports, so I came up with a policy called 'Get in the Game'.

It provided a yearly grant voucher of $150 that assisted up to 60,000 families each year with the cost of their children's sporting fees. Even today, the grant is still helping families each year, and it's such a delight to hear from mums, dads and carers, who appreciate the assistance.

Time Running Out To Get Sports Vouchers

February 24, 2014

Sport Minister Steve Dickson has urged Queenslanders to "get moving" on their Get Started grant applications, with Round 3 to end on Friday.

Get Started is one of three programs under the State Government's $47.8 million "Get in the Game" initiative which has been designed to help Queenslanders get active.

Mr Dickson said with demand under Round 3 had been nearly double that of Rounds 1 and 2.

Sport and Recreation Minister Steve Dickson

"Round 3 is well on track to being our biggest Get Started round yet, and is expected to help more than 20,000 children and young people join a sport or recreation club," Mr Dickson said.

"Due to the overwhelming demand, the round will be closing this Friday (February 28) so I strongly encourage families to apply as soon as possible.

"Vouchers are allocated on a first come, first served basis to eligible individuals, providing up to $150 to help pay club membership and participation fees.

"We have already seen some great results come through, with more than 25 per cent of successful applicants not having played club sport previously.

"We have also received an enormous response from clubs during this round of Get Started, with 3322 clubs now registered for the program, 48 of which registered just in the last month.

"Rugby league, soccer and netball clubs are proving the most popular for Round 3 vouchers so far."

Mr Dickson said the Queensland Government was keen to encourage more Queenslanders to get involved in sport and recreation.

"We made an election commitment to get more young Queenslanders involved in recreation and sport, and we are delivering through this highly successful program."

That same year, I established the first 'Women in Sport Committee' to help me form a policy concerning the needs of girls and women in sport. The first initiatives to be rolled out were change rooms for girls and designing the plans for a purpose-built netball centre at the Queensland Sport and Athletics Centre. The netball centre ended up being built by the next ALP sports minister.

Another initiative I launched together with a young Robert Irwin was called 'Nature Play', designed to get kids off devices and out into nature and the sunshine to exercise. We climbed a tree together. We weren't supposed to, it's illegal in Brisbane—believe it or not—but we did. He's a lovely young man and a wonderful role model for young Australians.

Having the racing portfolio paved the way for me to completely reforming Queensland's racing industry, with one of the biggest negotiated deals in its history, to support 30,000 jobs in the racing sector.

This ultimately led to a thirty-year wagering agreement and a $4.5 billion injection into the industry, to develop country racing and infrastructure. Before that, country racing in Queensland was in a terrible state. The bureaucrats wanted the racetracks closed to save money; however, the many conversations I had with the industry made it apparent that country racing was the lifeblood of many Queensland towns. Once they understood this, the government and Racing Queensland supported country racing to keep jobs and towns afloat.

Along with job creation, we had a good look at the infrastructure as well. One example of this was in Toowoomba. They had a synthetic racetrack that had proven to be a complete failure, so we investigated new options before laying a new $7 million grass track that was hugely successful. It made it safer for the horses and increased turnover for the bookmakers.

I filled in for Jack Dempsey for four weeks as the Police and Emergency Services Minister. During this time, I had the privilege of swearing in a group of police graduates, which was the highlight of my short time as minister. Each morning I would get a call from the Police Commissioner, Bob Atkinson, to fill me in on the latest events and it was never good news.

I don't know how the police, the minister, and all those involved coped with it day in and day out.

I have enormous respect and admiration for our resilient police force, brave fire fighters and emergency services personnel. Seeing them in action on Bribie Island, when the national park was alight, was incredibly inspirational and balanced out the darker side of the job. They were everyday people carrying out extraordinary activities, and heroes we should all be proud of.

Their bravery and sacrifice had an immense impact on me, so almost every Christmas since 2008, Deb and I have packed boxes with Christmas food, fresh scones and jam, coffee, pudding, cakes, drinks and decorations. We deliver the boxes to the local police station, fire station, ambulance centre and hospital emergency wards, early on Christmas morning. It is such a small gesture, but one we hope will remind them how much we appreciate their dedication to keeping us safe and saving lives.

Chapter 18

The road to ruin

The next state election occurred in 2015, and I was thrilled to win again with 52.62% of the primary vote. I was sworn into the 54th Parliament, but not in a ministerial role, as the LNP had lost government. Campbell Newman was no longer Premier of Queensland. Annastacia Palaszczuk had knocked him out of the top job and she was now leader of the Queensland Labor Government and Premier.

Just as Queensland was settling into life with a new government, Tropical Cyclone Marcia hit. There is nothing like a natural disaster to bring a community together. Politics were forgotten, as people pulled together to fill sandbags and protect each other's homes. The SES volunteers did a wonderful job. It is an organisation that all Australian's should be proud of.

After Newman's election loss, the LNP had reverted to Lawrence Springborg, as leader. He was put there to fill the space while others manoeuvred to replace him. Several groups were forming to make a takeover move on the leadership. It was only a matter of time before the LNP would have a new leader. In the meantime, all the supporters of the previous leader, including me, were relegated to the backbench—that's politics!

On May the 6th 2016, Tim Nicholls was elected leader of the LNP. Tim had to show loyalty to those who had supported his leadership bid, and as I hadn't supported him, I remained on the backbench, trying to earn back my stripes.

Party politics has never been about talent or work ethic; it's always about the numbers. This can be disappointing, personally, but it is something everyone in politics has to live with. It is a long-ingrained culture, which is in no way helpful for the state or country. Imagine if the right people, with the right skills and experience, were in the right roles in our government!

The LNP was going through many changes and there was a lot going on. Some of it was positive, but a lot left me shaking my head. I felt the party was beginning to make some questionable decisions and by the middle of 2016, my doubts had transformed into serious concerns that the LNP was heading way off-track. I kept thinking it was fixable; that is was nothing major—a small bump in the road they would see, fix and get back on track—but it was not to be the case.

Three major issues came up and it soon became apparent the party had not only gone off track but they were careening down it and spiralling out of control.

The taxi industry was in all sorts of strife because of the introduction of Uber, where drivers could just jump in a car without an expensive license and begin trading. However, mum and dad investors had paid the state government enormous amounts of money for their licenses and to set themselves up with jobs, often investing their whole life savings into the industry, and the LNP were abandoning them!

It just didn't make sense. A small number of LNP MPs, myself included, argued that our party should be supporting the taxi industry, not ignoring them or hiding behind some nonsense excuse the party had come up with.

The second ridiculous decision was not moving forward with the MRI (Mooloolah River Interchange), which would allow the coast road to function more effectively, by creating more roads that alleviated the existing pressure, in areas such as Mooloolaba, Mountain Creek, Kawana and Brightwater.

This was absolutely vital for residents and visitors to the Sunshine Coast. Local's major concern was that the interchange at Mountain Creek was unsafe because it caused vehicles to merge suddenly at high speed. The LNP knocked it on the head, saying that other areas were more important.

The Shadow Treasurer had advised me to 'hope' for the money to build the MRI, which to be honest shattered me. The Sunshine Coast was being overlooked because of our political successes, and now we weren't marginal enough—the seat was too 'safe'. Political parties in Australia are always reluctant to spend money in areas where their seats are relatively safe.

The third issue was not giving the green light for medicinal cannabis to be legally prescribed and used in our health system. Bec Bridson, a paramedic, had brought many people into my office to share their stories of how medicinal cannabis had improved their lives and to detail the medical relief it provided. The more they spoke about how it had transformed their lives, the more I could see how vital it was for people with serious medical conditions. There were hundreds of thousands of cases where people were using the black market for medical cannabis relief, but the LNP wouldn't hear of it.

I pushed hard on all three issues but couldn't get the support from the majority, which frustrated me immensely. As a result of my speaking out in the party room, the LNP leadership began ostracising me. It was subtle at first, and then undeniable when I was prevented from speaking to Bills within Parliament.

At first, I was put last on the speaking list for Bills and then taken off the list completely! I ripped into Trevor Watts, the current Whip, and called them all a bunch of back stabbers.

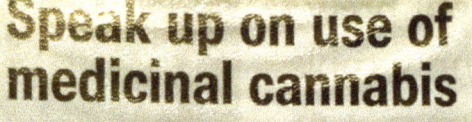

Speak up on use of medicinal cannabis

STATE SCENE
STEVE DICKSON MP

IN NOVEMBER 2015, I sponsored a Parliamentary petition calling for an amnesty relating to the use of medicinal cannabis.

This petition was signed by more than 13,000 Queensland residents in only 24 days. This gave me the mandate to pursue the implementation of a legislative framework for the legalisation of medicinal cannabis. I will be speaking on the Public Health (Medicinal Cannabis) Bill 2016 in the Queensland Parliament after the final report is received by September 30 and would like your assistance in gathering statistics on this important issue. I have launched a survey which can be completed at this link: www.goo.gl/qcxZx3.

Alternatively, you can complete the survey in person at my office at 102 Burnett St, Buderim. I will use this information for statistical purposes only. Your personal details will be kept confidential. The survey will close August 31.

Sadly, here we are in 2020, and the medical cannabis issue is still being hotly debated. People with chronic health problems still can't go to their local GP and get a prescription for whole plant medical cannabis or even CBD (Cannabidiol).

By then, I was extremely frustrated with the LNP. I didn't understand why they would not commit to funding the MRI or support the use of medical cannabis. They also refused to support the construction of the Bradfield Scheme, to drought-proof Queensland, but supported outrageous laws such as dropping the legal age of anal sex from 18 to 16 years for girls and boys. In my opinion it was totally unacceptable and a clear indication they had lost their way.

Chapter 19

Pauline

I began exploring ways to seek support from other parties, who could help deliver on what the community needed. I thought about Pauline Hanson and her comments about working with all levels of government, regardless of which party you belonged to. I couldn't see any other option, so I got in contact with James Ashby, Pauline's Chief of Staff to request a meeting with her.

James was well known as Pauline's right hand man—he totally dedicated to the newly elected senator, incredibly smart and very much on the ball. I thought the media gave him a raw deal, and from what I could see, it was unjustified. In my dealings with him, you always knew exactly where you stood, and he didn't make any excuses for focusing on and doing what was best for all Australians.

I soon learnt he was a guy, who always kept his promises and didn't tolerate fools. He had been instrumental in helping Pauline reform One Nation by vetting and bringing in more professional candidates from a variety of ethnic backgrounds. They had many people in the party without the political experience to win campaigns and, ultimately, seats. And without the seats, the party didn't have enough power to introduce the policies and change they wanted to see.

There were many people within One Nation, who did not like James, but I definitely wasn't one of them. I am sure they considered him a threat to their power base because of his tenacity, ambition and technical intelligence.

They were a party that was used to losing and they didn't like his drive, but Pauline saw his ability and the closer James got to Pauline the more unrest it caused in the party, until Pauline called for reform.

James locked in a time for Pauline to come to the Sunshine Coast and meet with me and he gave me a run down on what to expect from her. She had a mind of her own, didn't do bullshit or muck around wasting time, which was fine by me. I was looking forward to meeting her; she sounded like my kind of person.

I'd heard and read a lot about her—as we all have—and I was intrigued to meet her. Would she be the racist 'tin-foil hat' wearing person the media pegged her as.

What I did know was that, from a political point of view, she got things done and wasn't frightened of raising some of the more sensitive issues. I had to give credit where credit was due.

As Pauline held the balance of power in the federal Senate, it was an important visit for my electorate of Buderim. I was keen for her to see the number of issues that my area was facing first-hand, for example the lack of road infrastructure, and I wanted to discuss the MRI and how jobs could be created. She had great contacts within the federal government, so seeing the Sunshine Coast herself and going over the issues with her could only be positive for our region.

Pauline arrived for a meet and greet at my home in Buderim on October the 6th 2016, accompanied by James Ashby. I have to say, I was a little surprised by the woman I met. She was a genuinely nice person—easy to talk to, knowledgeable and very much in touch with what her community wanted. As a politician and a person, she impressed the hell out of me. Her passion, common sense and the research, data and information she had, astounded me.

After our initial meeting, we did a joint radio interview with 104.9 Sunshine FM—Buderim's local radio network and then we hit the road, so I could show her around our beautiful region. I discussed the issues with Pauline as we travelled, stopping here and there to introduce her to some of the people who were eager to talk to her about their problems and to get her thoughts on how she might address them.

Walking down the street next to Pauline was like being with a rock star—people streamed out of their homes and offices, wanting a photograph or to shake her hand. It was a sight to see. I'd never seen anything like it before and I can tell you that kind of thing didn't happen with the senators in the LNP.

As I watched her interact with the community, it quickly became apparent that people really liked her—they connected with her because she was real, genuinely listened and focused on what they had to say.

I took Pauline to see Urban Food Street, where 100 families work together over eleven streets to grow fruit and vegetables on their front verges. It is a fabulous idea that utilises otherwise vacant land and provides produce for the community. Pauline absolutely loved the concept and could not, for the life of her, understand why our local government wanted to plough it up. She was so worked up about it; she did a video on the spot ripping into our local council and asking how they could possibly want to destroy it.

Knowing Pauline was an advocate of men's mental health, I stopped to introduce her to members of the Buderim Men's Shed, another fantastic community facility, where men get together every week to talk about men's issues and health. Pauline was most impressed by the members' wonderful leather, wood and stained glass work and enjoyed meeting them all and listening to their community accomplishments.

Our next stop was the area where I had been fighting to implement the Mooloolah River Interchange. I was eager to show Pauline the problems there and demonstrate how badly an interchange was needed, as well as to discuss potential solutions. I had spoken about the MRI 20 times in the Queensland Parliament, through eleven questions on notice and in nine speeches to the Premier, Deputy Premier and the Minister for Main Roads. The infrastructure was urgently needed. It was a real showstopper, as far as solving traffic congestion in our region went, particularly with the new hospital development that was due to open in April 2017. Given the never-ending housing developments and the continual growth of tourism, our roads just wouldn't be able to handle the extra load. Pauline saw this first-hand and agreed it was essential. She did a video with me about it, which she posted on her Facebook page to highlight the issue.

En-route back to Buderim, we took a quick drive around the Sunshine Coast University and talked about the need for the Bruce Highway upgrade, as well as the North Coast Rail Duplication. Then, we met up with Adam Benjamin from Medifarm, to discuss medical cannabis, together with Bec, who had first brought the issue to my attention.

Dotted in between all these engagements Pauline squeezed in interviews with the Sunshine Coast Daily's editor Jenna Cairney, as well as Channel 7 and WIN. It was a jam-packed morning; she had definitely hit the ground running, and many would be hard-pressed to keep up with her.

We had a beautiful lunch at the Buderim Tavern, before racing off to our next scheduled meeting with Alistair Cook, the local chemist—a wonderful man who does a lot for the Buderim community. Following that, we headed back to my office where Pauline met with the Diggers Military Motorcycle Club. I was the only MP on the Sunshine Coast who would sit down and meet with them personally, which was deplorable. Pauline was able to hear from the returned servicemen and women about their issues with finding employment, places to live and suicide.

It's a terrible thing that more servicemen die of suicide than in active duty and Pauline felt the same as I did about these men and women who had put their lives on the line for our country and who had gotten bugger all in return. Pauline really championed these organisations, and she donated her weekly media fee from *Sunrise* to The Young Returned Veterans Association as well as to Meals on Wheels.

The more time I spent with Pauline, the more she impressed me. I could see where she was going politically. Her ethics and integrity were exceptional and some of her policies admirable.

The media covered Pauline's visit to the Sunshine Coast, with the news hitting both local and national news throughout the country. Pauline's comments, about infrastructure needs in the region were highlighted. This was fantastic, as it drew Parliament's attention to the issues, which was exactly what I needed. However, underneath the news stories was a subtext about why an LNP Member would invite the One Nation leader to the area? This planted the seed for others to question my motives, in public.

Chapter 20

Jumping ship

In Parliament, talk of the visit was on their minds, but not on the agenda. That didn't stop the premier from staging a Dorothy Dix question, "Why did the member for Buderim invite Pauline Hanson to his electorate instead of the leader of his own party?" This slyly introduced the unrelated topic and pulled it into that day's parliamentary discussion.

Pauline was impressed by what she had seen and heard on her trip to my electorate, and she made a statement to the media saying that her party would not run a candidate against me, for the seat of Buderim at the next election. Pauline said she believed I was doing a good job and representing the people well enough that a candidate wasn't needed there.

This statement inflamed my party even more and a ripple of talk questioned my motives further and began to flow out and into the media.

The Sunshine Coast Daily wrote an article, with a poll, on October the 13th 2016:

Premier Annastacia Palaszczuk has roasted Buderim MP Steve Dickson LNP for bringing One Nation Party head Senator Pauline Hanson to the Sunshine Coast to discuss infrastructure rather than his own party's leader.

Should Steve Dickson have brought an LNP leader to the Coast instead of Pauline Hanson?

15% Yes. His own party is in power in Canberra.

45% No. He should invite whomever he wants to.

38% If the Coast benefits I don't care who he invites.

The LNP were livid with this. As the gossip gained traction, and rumours began to fly about my 'close ties' with Pauline, the LNP made it clear that they didn't like it. I received a message from the leadership team's Chief of Staff asking me to attend a meeting with Tim Nicholls and his deputy, Deb Frecklington.

I barely had time to put my phone on the table, after walking into the room, before I was hit with a barrage of questions. Tim asked if I was going to leave the party, and Deb followed that up quickly, by accusing me of tape recording our meeting. I said, "No, I am not! Deb, you've been here five minutes and you are accusing me of secretly tape recording our meeting! Here's my phone I don't do that shit. And no Tim . . . I have had no intention of leaving the party."

I left that meeting, or perhaps interrogation would be a better description, with a lot of doubt. They had cast the first stone, but added to the concerns that I had already expressed that meeting was the moment I seriously thought my electorate could do better. Better than what we were getting through the LNP. Maybe it was time to look at other options.

Less than a month later, I had a meeting with Gary Spence, the Party President, to solve a problem that Sid Cramp, the member for Gaven was experiencing concerning pre-selection for his seat. Sid was a really nice bloke—someone you could trust—and he was also a strong supporter of the taxi industry and medical cannabis. Like me, he wasn't too impressed with the direction in which the party was heading and had his own doubts.

In my discussions with him, I got a clear warning that whatever was happening with him, as concerned his pre-selection, would also happen to me if I didn't tow the line. He emphatically believed he was being stitched up for going against the grain.

I'd already seen branch-stacking happening within the party. Parties would enlist large numbers of people from outside the party, to sign up for party membership, for one reason—to get rid of the sitting member. They did this by branch-stacking their pre-vote on to another candidate, whom they *did* want in office. It had already happened to Peter Slipper, a sitting LNP member on the Sunshine Coast—in fact, it was rife throughout the country.

State and Federal politics is a totally different arena from local council. Winning pre-selection for a party is all about the numbers that you get from the internal membership vote. If you get the membership onside you can win pre-selection, and from there you get the opportunity to run in the upcoming election.

Over the Christmas break I'd become really conflicted, and wondered if I could make any significant difference in Queensland politics, under the LNP. Our electorate never seemed to get its fair share of essential infrastructure, while ludicrous bills were being tabled all the time. I felt the party was being irresponsible with community needs and arrogantly throwing in policies that were nothing short of reckless.

I had delivered several major projects for the Sunshine Coast, as the Minister for National Parks, Recreation, Sport and Racing, but there was so much more to be done. However, I believed I had Buckley's chance of getting anything done while the party focused on the less marginal seats and ignored the Sunshine Coast, which had been loyal and had patiently waited for urgent infrastructure commitments from the LNP.

I weighed it up quietly for weeks. I knew it would be risky to jump ship. Firstly, I'd have to take a pay cut, so I worked out my budget to see if I could make that work. Then I thought about the connections I would potentially lose, if I was ostracised by my fellow parliamentary members and whether that would have an impact on my electorate in parliament, in the future.

Not everyone would understand why I'd changed parties, but the truth was that without change everything would have stayed the same. I had to take the risk for my community. I sat on it for a few more weeks, considering the move and thinking about the infrastructure that we so desperately needed here. I also considered those with chronic conditions, who wouldn't be able to access whole plant medical cannabis if I did nothing.

Obviously, I'd made a number of enemies with my stand on medical cannabis and my defence of the Queensland Taxi Industry, who in their darkest hours needed someone to champion them. I'd also been very vocal in opposing the lowering of the legal age limit for anal sex to 16, which honestly was just another outrageous decision of which I didn't want to be part.

I approached Pauline Hanson, personally, to ask if she would support my cause for whole plant medical cannabis, as well as a number of other issues, including support for the taxi industry, construction of the Mooloolah River Interchange and construction of a hybrid of the Bradfield Scheme. She said, "100% yes!"

Chapter 21

One Nation

After a thousand talks with Deb, the time had come. On January the 13th 2017, I left the LNP to join One Nation. The LNP had accused me of self-interest; my only interest was the people of the Sunshine Coast and their future.

To be honest, the odds of success were low—*really* low, but I believed the electorate and the people of Queensland deserved better. There was no glory in it for me, just a passion and a desire to deliver for my people. Something drove me on and my faith in God had never been greater.

Very soon after joining ON, Pauline asked me to take over the leadership role of the party in Queensland. I accepted the invitation, and on January the 24th 2017, I stepped into the role of Queensland leader of One Nation. I knew I had a huge job on my hands, managing candidates, writing policies and traveling extensively throughout the state—it was game on! This workload was in addition to my responsibilities as the member for Buderim, which was always my first priority.

I got down to business, launching our first policy: a hybrid of the Bradfield Scheme to drought-proof Queensland, which I announced on the day I became One Nation's leader. A week later I followed up with a commitment that, if elected and One Nation gained the balance of power in the Queensland Parliament, we would build the MRI I had been fighting for.

I shared the campaign trail with Michael Pucci, an American ex-Marine and ex-LNP Member of Parliament, who had been appointed One Nation's Campaign Director. He was a tremendous fellow and I got along really well with him. He did an outstanding job with the little resources and small support team that he had.

I wrote a twenty-one-point firearms' policy, to keep the current firearms laws in place, but streamlined them to amalgamate the different license categories into one, very much as driver's licences are today. This was done to assist struggling farmers, who felt they were being downtrodden by the government.

Along with the firearms policy, we wanted to re-establish the upper house of parliament in Queensland and to instigate a citizen-initiated referendum. This would give people the opportunity to vote on their ideas at any given election, provided it was supported. This potentially allowed for the legalising of medicinal cannabis or for changing other legislation, to give GPs the power to prescribe whole plant medicinal cannabis for patients in need.

I spent a great deal of time with Pauline, and even more time with James. You could often find us travelling and working throughout the state, even on weekends.

One Nation had a tiny budget compared to the ALP and LNP. We flew to Bundaberg in James's two-person, light aeroplane and, after we landed, we parked near premier, Annastacia Palaszczuk's, private ten-seater jet, which was HUGE. This alone showed me the complexity and enormity of the David and Goliath battle we had ahead of us.

We stayed in the cheapest hotel we could find, and then walked to the local pub where Paul Murray of Sky News was telecasting. I was on air thirty minutes after the premier. Paul's a top fella—smart and a good presenter—he certainly asked the hard questions. I liked him and did a number of interviews with him over the months leading into the election.

At that time, the sugar industry was facing a bleak future and it was difficult to see their plight up close. Wilmar, one of the biggest sugar mill owners in Australia, and the cane growers could not come to an agreement on price. Sam Cox, my deputy in North Queensland, was running for the seat of Burdekin. He was pushing for the government and opposition to back our plan to amend the Sugar Industry Act of 1999. The amendment would extend the current contract and provide an additional twelve months' negotiation time for Queensland farmers. The opposition and the government had failed the sugar cane industry—we were always fighting for the underdog—but as hard as we fought, the LNP and ALP continued to join forces to shut us down.

Back in Brisbane, Pauline would come into Parliament every now and then, which always mixed things up a bit. A stream of visitors would also drop in to say 'G'day', including some LNP members: Mark Robinson, the Member for Cleveland; Sid Cramp, the Member for Gaven; and Robbie Katter, the Member for Traeger in Central Queensland.

Robbie Katter and I had become good friends since my days as Sports Minister. Rob is one of the nicest politicians I have ever met. I trusted him and he trusted me and we had a good working relationship. Rob and I had worked together on a few things and we had struck a deal regarding the upcoming election. The One Nation Party would not run in two of the Katter seats and the Katter Party wouldn't run in Burdekin and Mirani; two of the seats One Nation were contesting. We also decided not to run against Jo-Ann Miller, in the seat of Bundamba; Mark Robinson, who was the Member for Cleveland; Leanne Linard, the Member for Nudgee; and Sid Cramp, the Member for Gaven. These MPs were hard-workers in their respective electorates, so we decided not to run candidates against them.

It was an extremely hectic time—meeting after meeting, and the parliamentary sittings and travel throughout the state just didn't stop. The debates between Annastacia Palaszczuk, Tim Nichols and me were also time-consuming.

I'd announced that One Nation would stop the $5.4 billion Cross River Rail project and reallocate that money to building a hybrid of the Bradfield Scheme. The scheme consisted of the construction of dams, channels, pipelines, and desalination plants, for watering purposes, using the best technology out of Israel. This project was all about drought-proofing Queensland and, ultimately, Australia as well.

Ironically, as of August 2020, the LNP in Queensland have taken the policy and claimed it as their own. When I brought it up in the party room, as a member of the LNP, they weren't at all interested. Back then, I felt building roads, railways, dams and a power station, fully funded by the savings made by scrapping the Cross River Rail project—which "only" benefited travellers by fifteen minutes— and was a much better use of the spend, and would benefit the community far more. It made sense, but they just couldn't see it.

We released our policy to support building the new Daniel Morcombe Centre in Palmwoods on the Sunshine Coast, working with Bruce and Denise Morcombe and we supported their policy to identify where paedophiles lived. It never came to fruition. It is incredibly difficult to understand why any party wouldn't support it! If a political party doesn't support this policy, then they must support these slimy, sick, disgusting individuals.

Leading up to the election, I didn't stop and neither did the phone. I checked in with James, a few times a day, and with Michael, the campaign director, along with helping and advising other candidates wherever I could.

On November the 25th 2017, I contested the seat of Buderim as the Queensland leader of the One Nation party ... and lost. I received 28.57% of the vote and the LNP candidate received 36.88%. All parties put One Nation last or second-to-last on the ballot, including the LNP, which swung it away from One Nation in the seat of Buderim.

I'm not going to lie; the loss was bloody hard to take. Losing the opportunity to deliver those three big initiatives was extremely disappointing and I felt as if I had let the community down. In addition to my main projects, I still had a big list of what I wanted to get across the line for my electorate, and for all Queenslanders.

Politics had always been about what I can do to help people. It still frustrates me to see 'seat warmers' in office; people who are only there for their own gain or to buy themselves a job for a few years. If you aren't there to improve your community, then move over and let someone, who's more driven, have a go.

After the election loss, I was also disappointed for my staff, Sheree, Dawn, Tony, Greg and Zak, as they had lost their jobs, too. They were all fantastic people, who worked really hard for our local community. Sheree was my Chief of Staff and she never stopped working.

There was no way I could have done my job without her support. Dawn also played a major role in running the office and looking after Buderim residents on a daily basis. Tony and Greg worked part-time, but their contribution was invaluable. Then there was Zak, a wiz with technology and video photography know-how and creativity.

The weeks after the election were spent cleaning out the office and the campaign house, sorting out loose ends, and taking a break for the couple of weeks leading up to Christmas. Life had changed so much. The phone stopped ringing, the pressure fell away, and I just wasn't sure what to do next.

Pauline invited Deb and me to visit her farm outside of Beaudesert, in early January, for a weekend of R & R and to get to know her and her partner better. She was a great host, cooking for us and making us feel at home, immediately. We discussed everything from Australia's future to why the bloody crows woke up so early on her property, and everything in between along with policies and the party.

Deb and Pauline got along very well. Deb's a very good judge of character and she liked Pauline. So did I. The thing that amazed me was how the media and other political parties kicked her around, jailed her, and said terrible things about her (many of them just lies) but she kept on going; she never wavered.

I believe I was in a fortunate position. Pauline trusted my judgment and she spoke openly to me. I trusted her, she trusted me, and we just clicked. We had many similar ideas and philosophies and we liked sticking up for the underdog and putting Australia and Australians first.

I was thrilled when Pauline asked me to be candidate number two on the senate ticket in Queensland for the next federal election, as well as to continue as leader of One Nation. This meant I would still be able to make a difference when it came to the community and it would keep my name in the public arena for the next election.

It also gave me the opportunity to work with candidates and party members.

I became Pauline's senior advisor, which kept me in the loop in Canberra, and I attended meetings, worked on policies and was part of her team. For this, I will always be grateful.

Who knows if it was in our DNA or just the redhead in us both, but we thrived on thinking of outside the box for solutions and worked well together because of it. We didn't always agree, but she would listen to an argument, before forming an opinion and that was good enough for me.

I felt fate had played its trump card in having us meet and work together. It seemed we were bound to meet eventually, as we had several points in life—including attending the same high school—where we could have met each other earlier; but this seemed to be our time. It was great to be working with her.

Chapter 22

The senate

In February 2018, I flew to Canberra. This time I was put up in a hotel, as an advisor to Senator Hanson, instead of sleeping in my car as I had done thirty-odd years earlier as a backpacker.

The trip involved meeting after meeting. I'd arrive at work by 7am, have breakfast in the café, and then get stuck into work for the day and well into the night. I had meetings with the medical cannabis representatives and Malcolm Roberts, on the lawn of federal parliament, while they were protesting and trying to gain the attention of the politicians, the public and the media.

When we were in Canberra for senate work, we had strategy meetings, to discuss the bills that were before the house that day and which of them One Nation would support in parliament. Pauline always asked everyone in attendance what their opinions were—I couldn't help myself and I often spoke up about the things I believed were important and that were still outstanding on my wish list for my community.

The two other Senators were Brian Burston and Peter Georgiou. Brian was a friendly, but secretive man, who didn't really understand the opportunities he had by speaking in the senate.

He could have used them more to benefit his constituents and their issues. I wrote a speech, with Malcolm Roberts, for Brian on why some politicians and sportsmen need to cheat. It was around the time of the Australian cricket teams' sandpaper incident in Newlands, Cape Town. I suggested to Brian that he get a cricket ball and throw it up and down as a bit of tongue-in-cheek humour, to lift the exposure of his speech in the media. Some days, you had to pull out a few stops to be noticed. Well, he took my advice, the media loved it, and the speech got the outcome he wanted.

Peter Georgiou was new to the political world, as well. He'd only been in the senate since the 27th of March 2017. I really liked Peter, he was a businessman in his former life and he was one of those guys you could rely on to deliver. He wasn't a polished politician, by any means, but that's what the country needed—men and women just like him: regular, passionate, down-to-earth listeners and doers.

I worked with Peter a lot and as each sitting went by, he got better at assimilating the knowledge and confidence needed to become a fantastic senator. He took a great interest in the Western Australian gas tenements, which had been capped for many years. Peter continued to fight for these tenements to be used for domestic purposes, as well as calling for the federal government to create a 'use it or lose it' policy. He was also responsible for delivering an MRI machine to Kalgoorlie and $3 million for Football WA.

I couldn't say the same about Brian, especially after he decided to join Clive Palmer's party. He began to throw around a series of wild stories and accusations in the media, including one where he had a shot at Pauline for supposedly propositioning him; a story, which was so far-fetched I don't think anyone took him seriously.

After that pearler, he went on to accuse James Ashby of starting a fight with him, in the Great Hall of Parliament House, which was totally untrue—I was there and saw the whole thing.

Rod Messenger and Mick Bainbridge, a returned serviceman, and I had been in a meeting in Pauline's office, that evening, when James asked me to come down to the Great Hall. He wanted me to accompany Pauline and him back to the office, as there was a controversial issue erupting because of Brian's accusations about Pauline in the media. I couldn't leave Rob and Mick in the office, so I brought them with me.

The Australian newspaper asked James if they could get a photo of Pauline, coming out of the Great Hall, so they could use it in a story they were running about the accusation. James was about five metres away from Mick, Rob and me, taking these pictures, when Brian and his wife walked out of the Hall. James took a photo of them, and Brian lost it, going for James before grabbing his phone and throwing it across the floor; all the while hurling abuse at him.

For reasons no one—except him—knows, he went to Pauline's office and smeared blood down her door, which he admitted to in parliament the next day. It was an absolute debacle. Mick, Rob and I can all confirm that James never laid a hand on him.

Pauline copped a lot of unnecessary rubbish. Some people were relentless in their drive to take her down, but she just kept going as always. God, she had some tenacity, and was driven by sheer passion and purpose.

She did the right thing by many—most actually—and she remembered people in need. The Buderim Men's Shed—one of the initiatives I'd had on my list for years and where I'd taken Pauline some years earlier—was given $500,000, to complete their project to build a new men's shed to house 300 members, their machinery and so forth, in a directive from Pauline. The decision to grant the Shed the money was decided in a matter of minutes, in an opportunity that arose under the discretion of Mathias Cormann in Parliament. It's amazing what you can do in Canberra.

When I wasn't on the road, or in Canberra, I loved being at home with Deb and catching up with the boys who were 31 and 29 years old by then and working in council and accounts respectively.

Deb and I would start our day as we had always done. We'd get up at 4am, have brekky together and go through our morning routine. Deb scanned the social media sites, to make sure none of the candidates were doing anything stupid and kept us informed of everyone's happenings, so I could follow up on anything that might affect the party.

With our daily system in place, we made a great team. It was terrific for Deb because she was up to date on everything that was going on within and outside of the party and it helped me keep my finger on the pulse. It helped to know the community's needs, issues and concerns, so I could deliver a solution or address any issues raised.

I travelled a lot; from the Sunshine Coast to Canberra, Perth, Sydney, and Brisbane, as well as going up and down the east coast of Queensland, meeting with people and getting out and seeing problems first-hand.

In Innisfail, I went to a meeting about the implications of the Vessel Monitoring System (VMS), which was effectively bringing the fishing industry to its knees and was a bureaucratic cost that these people just couldn't afford. There had to be 50 fishing families at that meeting, who were crying out for someone to listen to them; someone who would genuinely care about their livelihood. Unfortunately, the Labor Party continued to pursue their policy, regardless of the effects on the local fishing industry.

Chapter 23

The foreign agent

Life was busy but good until June the 9th 2018, when it all came to a grinding halt. That was when I came into contact with the man who would change our lives in the most horrific way possible.

You'd think that, given the career I was in, there would be a lot of shonky characters, and there were definitely a few that fit the bill, but on the whole I not only met but became friends with many down to earth, hard-working people who were in government for all the right reasons.

More often than not, you could see the shady ones coming from a mile away. I was no dummy when it came to people and Deb was even sharper than I was, but there was one man who not only completely slipped under our radar but he also shattered our world.

A month earlier, on May the 5th, James asked me to call a guy named Rodger Muller, whom James had met in New South Wales and who wanted to learn about One Nation's firearms' policy. This was no different from a thousand requests we received regularly. Usually Pauline, James or I would meet with anyone, from fishermen to farmers and every group in between, to discuss all manner of issues. On the surface this was like all the other simple requests for a meeting—nothing more, nothing less.

When I called James, to get an overview of what it was all about, he said he'd met Rodger at the One Nation launch in NSW, and that he was from an organisation called Gun Rights Australia.

Rodger had asked James if Pauline could make a short video that he could use on his online media outlet, about One Nation's policy on firearms and the benefits of streamlining the firearms' licence process in the same way as drivers' licences are handled. Pauline's schedule was full, but I had created the firearms' policy, so I was asked to run him through our policies and do a bit, to camera, for his Facebook/online video—easy!

I gave Rodger a call the next day. He seemed like an ordinary guy, as he told me how me he wanted to learn more about One Nation's firearms policy. He was verbally passionate about protecting Australian gun laws, to make sure they were not watered down or made more difficult for sporting shooters or farmers.

It was a thought-provoking conversation and he seemed legit to me. His thoughts and views matched those of One Nation, which included:

- Legislate for a general firearms amnesty for any person who wishes to surrender a firearm, or register an unregistered firearm.
- Streamline the current system of firearms' licensing, to make legitimate gun ownership less costly and convoluted.
- Standardise all firearm licenses to a ten-year renewal, with no increase in fees.
- Review the Weapons Act, and Regulations and Weapons Categories Regulations, in consultation with all stakeholders and industry experts within the first year of forming government.

The focus of the policy is to move away from trying to criminalise firearm ownership to punishing criminals for using firearms to commit crimes. The details of the policy include:

1. Recognise that as a matter of principle, licensed firearm ownership by law-abiding citizens is a right in a free society. More focus towards causal factors in gun violence including criminal use of firearms, mental health issues and support for policing violent domestic situations.

2. Create a general unregistered firearms amnesty involving dealers, with both the opportunity to surrender unregistered firearms and the opportunity for licensed shooters to register them without penalty.

3. Introduce a Licence Instant Verification System (LIVS) for firearm dealers to replace the current paper-based PTA system to ensure firearms are not sold to those whose licence is cancelled or expired.

4. Create a single firearms licence system with multiple endorsements for specific uses (e.g. collector, dealer, handgun, security guard, etc.), to avoid the requirement for multiple licences for occupational shooters.

5. End the so-called 'genuine reason/genuine need' test for each individual firearm on the basis that the licensed individual has already been cleared a fit and proper person to possess a firearm in any given category he/she is licensed for.

6. Reduce waiting periods before purchasing handguns in line with the 28-day waiting period for other firearm categories, and initial purchase reduced to three instead of six months whilst maintaining the three participation matches currently required. No compulsory waiting period for any second or subsequent firearms, as this serves no logical purpose other than to inconvenience shooters.

7. Remove the provisions restricting firearms based on subjective appearance and adhere to the measurable categories of functionality as per the Australian customs import test.

8. Ensure that primary producers and feral pest controllers continue to be able to use categories A, B, C, D and H firearms.

9. Exempt calibre, barrel length and magazine restrictions for state and national competition shooters to allow the re-establishment of international shooting competitions, which have been largely destroyed by the current restrictions.

10. Allow the purchase of ammunition for firearms outside of the existing licence category to cater for borrowing a registered firearm from another licensed owner, for example when assisting pest control on their property (reasonable excuse).

11. Legalise volunteer feral pest controllers to assist in eradication of severe feral infestations on rural properties and promote this within DPI and the EPA.

12. Make membership lists for gun clubs legally exempt from requests to access or view by external parties without a warrant, including other members, to prevent criminals or anti-firearm extremists gaining access to this information.

13. Introduce intelligence-based licensed firearm owner audits to free-up police hours. Police to be encouraged to educate licensed firearm owners about firearm security, rather than attempt to penalise unintentional minor mistakes.

14. Reduce the requirement for pistol owners to shoot in a minimum number of competitions each year for each category of firearms owned. On the basis that this provides no safety benefit and is simply an onerous bureaucratic requirement akin to requiring that a driver travel a minimum number of kilometres per year in order to keep a driver's licence.

15. Recognise recreational hunting and pest control as legitimate reasons to obtain a firearms licence with no landholder letter required.

16. Authorise sports shooting associations and clubs that wish to teach firearms licence safety courses.

17. Reduce police firearms storage verification if a shooter can on initial inspection show that they exceed the safe storage requirement (dual locking, Dyna bolting, multi-bolt safe doors). Introduce a signed acknowledgement of the requirement for safe storage of firearms in compliance with the relevant legislation for those purchasing their first firearm, including an acknowledgement of the penalty for failing to comply with this.

18. Allow licence applications, changes and renewals to be undertaken online as well as at police stations and firearms dealers.

19. Mandate performance benchmarks for weapons licensing to dispatch new and renewed licences within 30 days of application being delivered to Weapons Licensing Branch. Recognise in law that receipt of an application for renewal of an expiring firearms license extends licence validity until the receipt of the new firearms licence.

20. Introduce increased accountability and transparency for firearms regulators under the Weapons Act to ensure that powers are clearly defined in law and limited to specific situations to avoid arbitrary decision-making.

21. Introduce significantly increased penalties for crimes committed with a firearm and theft of a firearm.

Satisfied with what he was requesting, I locked in a time for a month later, when he and a small film crew would come up to my Sunshine Coast home and discuss the policy and make the short video interview on behalf of One Nation.

Chapter 24

Setting the stage

On May the 10th, James texted Rodger Muller saying, "Hi Rodger, did you speak to Steve Dickson?" Rodger responded, "Hi James, I had a really constructive conversation with Steve on Sunday morning. We are definitely on the same page and have started the bones of the plan. I'll keep you in the loop."

One month and three days later, on June the 9th, Rodger and the film crew arrived at our home. I had just finished cleaning up around the property and Deb was organising lunch and some afternoon tea. They arrived late. Rodger Muller was slightly overweight in appearance and looked every bit as one might imagine a gun rights' activist to look in his country-style shirt, brown jacket and extra-large Akubra hat. While the young cameraman juggled his equipment, Rodger introduced himself and the rather plain-looking woman with him as Diana Armatta, his personal assistant. Diana reminded me of the Girl Guide leaders you saw in films from the 60s, her long hair was tied up in a ponytail, and she wore thick glasses, khaki pants and a shirt that was belted at the waist.

We invited them in to take a seat at our dining room table and to have something to eat before we started. As Deb served up lunch, Rodger spoke about his love of Australian products and began recounting stories of Aussie battlers who had made good—the more he talked, the louder he got; he had a BIG personality.

I'd looked up Gun Rights Australia on Facebook and his website beforehand, to get an indication of what his organisation was all about and what he stood for. If nothing else, you could tell that Rodger had strong opinions and wasn't backward in coming forward about them. He loved to name-drop. In the course of telling his stories about Aussie battlers, he also emphasised his love of America, and he related numerous tales about high-profile people with whom he had regular dealings.

It appeared to both Deb and me that the guy knew everyone there was to know in the States. He spoke endlessly about Donald Trump Junior; he must have brought his name up at least a dozen times! He told us about attending a function with Trump Jr., where a large albino python slithered freely across the lawn while tigers in cages watched it and the delegates.

He knew all the tricks of the trade, when it came to fundraising and computer-oriented campaigning, through his involvement with governors and senators. He told us he could connect us with the right people who could teach One Nation some strategies that would be helpful in future campaigns. It was enlightening. We hadn't heard of most of the campaigning tactics he talked about, let alone tried or implemented them in Australia.

During the lunch, my phone kept pinging with messages or ringing with incoming calls. I excused myself to go into my home office and returned a few calls, while Rodger, Diana and Deb continued to talk. Deb told me later that night that Rodger had asked her many questions about our life, including our travels to overseas destinations such as Bali, Phuket, Hong Kong and Taiwan.

He also asked about my upbringing and political career as well as how we had met. Deb told him the story of our amazing 32 years of marriage and spoke about how hard I always worked.

When I returned to the room, Deb and Rodger were having a laugh at my expense, as Deb recounted the story of me as a sixteen-year old lad heading off to live with my dad in the Philippines, and about how I had dated a movie star—albeit for a few weeks. She loved that bloody story and always had a laugh telling it! I wanted to know more about Rodger, so I asked him about his life. He told us he was also happily married, and had two children.

Diana said she was separated from her husband, who was in the USA, and she now lived in Australia with her young daughter. Rodger had apparently employed her to work for Gun Rights Australia doing his website, tech, booking his meetings, etc., with Rodger adding that she was his 'go to' person. Rodger again referenced the USA and said he would love to put us in touch with his connections, as the opportunities for One Nation would be terrific.

With time ticking away, I was keen to get the video done, so we got the ball rolling as Deb cleared away the afternoon tea dishes. Rodger asked the young cameraman to pick the right spot in the garden to set up his equipment, while Rodger briefed me on what was to be said in the video. I had no problem talking about and reciting our firearms' policy—it was available on the One Nation website for the world to see and I had already done a similar video for the Shooters' Union.

Once filming was out of the way, we returned to the house and I suggested we head up the hill to the Buderim Tavern for a meal and a beer. Deb decided to stay home, as she was keen to finish off one of her craft projects, so I jumped into my car with Rodger, while Diana and the cameraman followed in their own car, so they could head straight back to Brisbane afterwards.

We spent another hour or two talking, enjoying a beautiful meal and taking in the spectacular view of the Sunshine Coast, which is quite a sight from the tavern's back deck. Rodger continued to talk about Donald Trump Jr, as well as some friends and acquaintants he had in the National Rifle Association (NRA) and other major companies and organisations. He certainly told a colourful story, including how he was outside the Lindt Café in Sydney when terrorist, Man Harmon Monis, killed two innocent people and stopped the city in its tracks.

I was intrigued when he spoke about the upcoming Congressional Sportsmen's dinner that was to be held in the States, and how he'd love Pauline to go with him to meet some of the senators and congressmen he'd been talking about—possibly even President Donald Trump. He seemed to be legitimate in my opinion, so on my way out of the tavern I asked him to send through a request for Pauline to attend and I'd pass it on to her PA.

On the drive back home, I called James from the car to let him know Rodger would contact him about Pauline's possibly going to the USA. After that call, I didn't think about Rodger much more—my workload was full. It was in James and Pauline's hands now so I moved onto the next call, meeting or issue I had to solve.

Rodger followed his request with an email to Pauline. James responded to this on July the 10th, saying that although Pauline would love to attend, she was far too busy with other commitments at the time. Maybe she could attend next year.

Rodger replied, saying he was on the road, but found that very disappointing news. He went on to say, "I understand her political requirements with an election looming, but is there any way we could make this work?"

He had apparently lined up some key players, who were very excited about meeting Pauline. They were impressed by her and saw her importance in Australia's future.

Rodger was tenacious, and asked, "What if we can shorten the trip and schedule a compressed two-day agenda?" He said it had taken him years to build these relationships, so he didn't want to mess up their schedules and he believed all parties could benefit greatly by working together.

James responded saying he understood, and asked if there was any use in either me, as a senior advisor, or Stephen Andrews, the Member for Mirani, attending on Pauline's behalf. Rodger said that could be an option and he would discuss it the following day, but that he really wanted Pauline's star power at the event.

Chapter 25

The long haul

With Pauline unable to make the USA trip, it was decided that Stephen Andrews would be a good replacement. He was a current, elected Queensland representative who also owned a gun supply business, therefore he knew a lot about farmers' needs in relation to firearms.

However, just a few weeks out from the trip, Stephen had to pull out of the trip as the dates clashed with his having to be in Parliament. James asked me to go with him instead. I was thrilled at the opportunity! I'd never been to the USA and was excited to get the opportunity. The One Nation head office footed the bill for airfares, accommodation and transfers, so all I had to do was provide my own spending money—it was to be the trip of a lifetime.

Rodger's office had planned a fantastic itinerary, which he gave to James and me personally on August the 27th, in Pauline's senate office, at Waterfront Place in Brisbane. Rodger had organised the whole trip and had booked all the meetings we were to have with the NRA and Koch Industries, as well as tickets for us to attend the Congressional Sportsman's Foundation's Annual Dinner and Banquet where James would deliver a three-minute speech. He also said there was a good chance of meeting President Trump, senators, congressmen, and other business people, as well as a possible meeting with the National Shooting Sports Foundation.

The four weeks leading up to the trip to the USA were hectic. The Longman by-election had just been held; Pauline was away on an overseas trip she'd booked a year earlier and I was running from pillar to post, having meetings and doing interviews for Sky News, about killing off any further tax breaks for multinationals and the banks. I also came out against being dictated to by the UN, regarding our intake of immigrants.

With only ten days until I flew out to the States, my schedule was still very busy. I met representatives from the Dairy Farmers of Victoria, who were doing it pretty tough, regarding water use and their rights to water. Pauline and I also met up with many others, including union reps and children with Type 1 diabetes. Pauline was really taken with these children—she always showed such genuine compassion. It was also an issue close to my heart, as my dad had died from the effects of diabetes, so we were very keen to help them in any way possible.

I returned home on the 24th, to help Deb, who had run over a log with her car. It was great to be home. It gave me a chance to catch up on some work, to do some maintenance on our property—which Deb had being doing the lion's share of—and tick off some more routine jobs such as get a haircut and visit the dentist.

The next couple of days were loaded with videos, calls, liaising with candidates, cleaning up and ticking off as much as I could, before I briefly touched base with Rodger on August the 27th, at Pauline's office. James and I went over the final itinerary with him and I said was looking forward to visiting Washington, D.C., learning about political marketing and, hopefully, getting the opportunity to meet Donald Trump Jr., or even the president himself.

I had been working really long hours and even during the brief time at home, I was on the run, trying to pull my weight. I was getting more tired, but I didn't have the time to entertain it, as I still had one more engagement to go before heading overseas.

I flew out to Birdsville for a couple of nights, for the Birdsville Cup, with Pauline, James and some fantastic One Nation supporters and business people. We left Brisbane at 9am, and arrived in time to attend the famous Birdsville  Races, before heading off to the equally famous Fred Brophy's Boxing Troupe event. We finished the day off with a very late dinner with a great bunch of people.

Pauline was the centre of attention everywhere we walked, with people flocking to her to say hi, to shake her hand, give her a hug or get a photo. It was as if a celebrity had flown into town.

 That night, all of us—including Pauline—bedded down in swags on the ground around the fire, under the stars. James, Pauline and I, and some big hitters, were all on the same level and we had a great conversation before getting some sleep. It was a great way to round off a busy two weeks of sittings in Parliament, the marathon, interviews, meetings, numerous calls and emails.

Exhaustion hit me after a combination of a whirlwind few months and a lack of sleep. Sleeping on the rocky ground at Birdsville had done me no good at all—I felt every bit of my age as I drove back to the Sunshine Coast that day. When I arrived home, looking weathered and like something the cat had dragged in, I saw the worry through Deb's smile. She was less than impressed with me having to go off again within hours, but she pushed through it with her usual big beautiful smile. She grabbed my dusty bag and put the washing on.

Deb helped me pack my bags again that same day, ready for the trip to Sydney and then the States. She chatted away all the while filling me in on what was happening at home with our family and friends.

I can't tell you how lucky I've been to have a partner such as Deb. As well as being my best friend, she's always been incredibly supportive of me, and everything I've done. While I travelled all over the place for work, she kept the ship steady, the boys happy, and maintained our household of two-and-a-half acres. That afternoon I kissed Deb goodbye and with my passport, itinerary of meetings, plane tickets and bags, I was back on the road—America bound!

After dropping my car at James' house, I arrived back at the Brisbane Airport just under six hours after I had left it that morning. As One Nation was picking up the travel bill, I converted $1000 of my personal funds to USD700 and caught the plane to Sydney, to meet up with James, before flying on to Los Angeles the next day.

After I landed in Sydney, I went straight to the Mercure Hotel where James and I had been booked in for the night, before the early morning departure to the International Airport. I didn't even catch up with James that night; I went straight to my hotel room and conked out. I was dead to the world until 4am, when my alarm went off.

I was up and ready to go, with my bags packed, when I called Deb at 5:45am, to say good morning as I did every morning when I was away. Then I met up with James and we headed to the airport.

Poor James looked as shattered as I felt. We boarded the plane for the long-haul flight to LAX at 9:15am. We were lucky; we'd been upgraded into business class, which was a real treat. Settling into my seat, I closed my eyes as exhaustion overcame me. I barely remember listening to the flight attendant's safety demo and within minutes, I was fast asleep.

Chapter 26

USA

The flight over the Pacific was relaxing; I drifted in and out of sleep for a while before hearing a noise behind my seat. I turned to see a couple of blokes at the bar having a chat about travelling to the US, to do a deal for cheap gas in Australia—something to do with a fertiliser business, which intrigued me. I approached them and had a chat, learning about their business venture, while having a couple of Scotches, before going back to my seat and sleeping again.

I woke in time to watch the sunrise, as we entered US airspace, before finally touching down on American soil at 8:20am. We disembarked from the international flight and changed to a domestic link, to fly through to our destination of Washington, D.C. We arrived while it was still daylight, at 5pm.

Straight away, two things struck me as extraordinary. One was witnessing the remarkable respect Americans have for their service men and women, who were given the right to board first at every gate, and which I thought was fantastic. The other was the number of American flags everywhere—not just in the airport—but everywhere we travelled. America is an incredibly patriotic country and it's heart-warming for even a foreigner to see that.

Rodger and Diana met us at the airport, along with a friendly, surfer-looking fella from California, called Colin. Rodger had organised for Colin to be our driver and to transport us to our hotel. By 5:17pm, we were in the car taking in familiar sights that I'd only ever seen in the movies or on TV. These included the Washington Monument, a truly spectacular obelisk made of marble, granite and bluestone gneiss; the National Museum of African American History and Culture, which had only been opened officially two years earlier by then-President Barack Obama; and the architecturally impressive Capitol Building, home of the US Congress.

As we drove past the White House, the reality of the situation began to sink in, and I was quite overwhelmed. I couldn't believe a farm boy from Gelobera was in the capital of the free world, taking in such significant attractions.

Before we knew it, we had arrived at our hotel. I checked into room 578 at the Hyatt, a clean, tidy hotel that was maybe a little on the dated side, but with reception staff who were friendly and welcoming.

Once in my room, my first port of call was to phone Deb to let her know we had arrived in Washington, D.C., safe and well. We chatted for a couple of minutes about the flights and what was going on back home. I couldn't wait to have a good shower after the 22 hours of travel we'd just had—gee it was good! I unpacked my luggage and ironed some clothing, before racing off to meet Rodger at the bar in the lobby. I pretty much left the room as quickly as I had entered it.

We joined Rodger and Diana at a table near the window for a drink and something to eat. We chatted easily about our flight and our first impressions of the US, over a couple of beers.

Rodger, a businessman from Shoalhaven Heads, talked about the trips he had made to America over the past few years, and how well the US economy was going. As he told it, his latest business, a dog food called 'Man's Best', was thriving back in Australia. He had been involved in a number of businesses with his wife, Alison, including turf, fruit and vegetable companies, and delivering medical supplies— he seemed to have a wealth of experience.

Rodger told us that it was highly likely that President Trump would be the special guest at the congressional dinner we planned to attend, which was exciting news and we hoped it was true! Rodger said that the year before he'd sat at Donald Trump Jr.'s table and, since meeting him, they had crossed paths a couple of times at other functions.

As the night wore on, the effects of the long flight and the few drinks hit James and I, and we were keen to hit the hay (in hindsight we should have), but Rodger began ordering us Scotches, which prompted a second wind and we kicked on for a while longer. Rodger began chatting about One Nation and the upcoming election, asking us how much we would need to run an effective election campaign in Australia.

At the time, I thought he was very passionate—his questions about Australian politics, our firearms' policies etc., were relentless. He told us that he had even run for the Senate in NSW, to get his own policies through, and spoke about what it had cost him in addition to the time and energy. He was throwing out numbers all over the place. To us, it seemed as if he knew a whole lot more than we did about campaigning. Rodger was so passionate and keen to know everything about the party and be involved that I thought he was going to tell us he wanted to run for One Nation!

James and I were three sheets to the wind by this stage; neither of us was big drinkers and as sometimes happens when you get a group of guys together with too much Dutch courage we got a bit silly and started throwing random numbers around. I said "$10 million" and James said, "No, it would be more like $20 million, to be really competitive with the ALP, LNP, the Greens, *and* Clive Palmer." Who honestly knew, it could have been $500 million for all we really knew.

It was well after midnight when we pulled up and called it a night. It was great evening—easy and relaxed, and we had some laughs and swapped stories over many, many drinks. I had enjoyed it, until the bill arrived: USD750—I nearly choked. Seven-hundred-and-fifty US dollars for the three of us! I should have taken Diana's lead. I can't remember her having a drink all evening. I'd never been involved in such a bloody expensive drinking session in all my life! I rarely drink, so I guess it was a rookie error, which I should have learned from, but I didn't. Pulling out my USD250 share, I was grateful we had stopped when we did or I'd be living on beans for the remainder of the trip.

As we left the restaurant to head back to our hotel room, neither James nor I looked for or noticed anything out of the ordinary, but if we had, we may have noticed the secret camera set up outside the window that had been filming us for who knows how long.

Chapter 27

The NRA

A little dusty after too many drinks the night before and still jet-lagged, I got up, phoned Deb and was ready to go by 8:15am. I had some breakfast downstairs and likely one of the worst coffees I've had in my life, from Starbucks—it was bloody terrible!

By 9am, we were driving the forty minutes to the headquarters of the National Rifle Association in Virginia, to meet the representatives Rodger was keen for us to see during our visit. The NRA was founded in 1871, by Col. William C. Church and Gen. George Windgate. It is a very sharp operation with around 5.5 million members and it pulls in a whopping $170 million in fees every year.

The drive was enjoyable and it was interesting seeing all the flags and monuments as well as the houses, which were quite different to those in Australia. The weather was similar to Queensland at that time of year. Everything was very lush and green.

As we arrived into Virginia, you couldn't miss the NRA headquarters—a huge white building with lots of glass. It was something you would never see on the Sunshine Coast. It had a collection of its own internal office buildings over several levels and housed a café, a firing range and a museum. It was a very professional facility.

We arrived with almost ninety minutes to spare, which gave us the chance to walk through the National Firearms' Museum, one

of the biggest firearms' museum in the world. As an Australian country boy, who had grown up always having a rifle and watching all the old country and western movies, I was very excited to be amongst so much history. We all have hobbies and interests and I was in my element, much like a car enthusiast at a car show.

I saw the handgun that was owned by JFK, as well as Princess Diana's personal guns. They also had Annie Oakley's shotgun and pistols; the handguns used by Clint Eastward in the *Dirty Harry* movies and all of the firearms Charlton Heston and John Wayne had used in their movies. If there was ever a famous firearm, it was pretty certain you'd see it in that museum. I was so impressed that I made a video on what I had seen, which I eagerly posted to my Facebook page for everyone to see.

We met up with Rodger for our meeting with the communications and strategic planning executive of the NRA, Lars Dalseide, a nice fella in his 40s. Lars was well versed across a range of topics and an absolute guru when it came to all things media. We also met Catherine Mortensen, who was also in her 40s.

Catherine was just as friendly as Lars was, and she generously shared anything we wanted to know about the NRA.

We asked them many questions, including how they went about their marketing and how they reached out to constituents and the public through education and public relations. I was interested to know how they handled difficult situations in the media, given the particular societal division between those in the pro and anti-gun lobby in the USA.

Lars spoke to us about the way the media continually gives the NRA a hard time and how they deal with it head on. He said they represented regular firearms owners—farmers and people just like me. He also talked about the second amendment (the people's right to keep and bear arms), which is part of the United States' Constitution. I found him to be a very reasonable person and certainly not one of those over the top people portrayed on television.

Lars and Catherine told us how they communicate the NRA's message via newspapers and the media, and through their social media sites, using six-second video grabs that work really well for engaging the general public. They created strategies based on their experience in developing print, online and social media content, and they wrote speeches and op-eds for community influencers, law enforcement and elected officials. By engaging communications and strategic planning, they possessed a winning blend of subject matter expertise, relationship management and practical experience.

The NRA was all over it. They leveraged a unique mix of strategic and analytical expertise and consistently exceeded their performance goals, by aligning their talents and effort with their organisational objectives regarding messaging, public relations and media relations.

Catherine said that both she and Lars had advanced through a series of positions at the NRA, including Senior Media Specialist, Communications Manager, Media Manager, and Media Liaison and Spokesman, to serve key roles in shaping the development of public policy and perception concerning constitutional rights in the United States. Together they oversaw a team that developed original content for publication and syndication on a daily basis, as well as social media, digital media, newsletters and press kits.

In addition to all of that, they also worked hard to form relationships with key stakeholders and state and national reporters, to ensure that they received accurate information. These relationships also resulted in the NRA's viewpoint being fairly presented in controversial news articles in state and national media publications, which really impressed us. Having just one on-the-record spokesperson for the group meant they were able to reduce the chance of false narratives and miscommunication being disseminated to the public.

The NRA had used this media approach to create a 400-plus-member surrogate program, which had led to coverage from the New York Times, CBS, Time, Fox and CNN. This resulted in a 150% increase in public opinion about their Nevada ballot initiative and an increased social media engagement of 400–600%.

They were very generous in sharing their knowledge. We learnt a lot from them and I was excited to take some of their proven strategies home to share with our team in Australia.

After our meeting, they took us on a tour of their indoor shooting range, which was a first for me—I'd only ever seen outdoor ranges. It wasn't open to the public when we were there, however we did get to speak with the fellow who ran it. He explained that they mainly held classes in the afternoons and evenings. Their students were predominantly women, learning how to use firearms safely.

He also said they had many young people who came in to learn how to clean and maintain their firearms. They also ran shooting competitions, as the sport was growing in popularity right across the USA.

It was late in the day when we sat down to have lunch at the building's café and met with another bloke Rodger had lined up for us. He was an NRA research attorney by the name of Christopher Zealand. Christopher spoke about much of the same kind of stuff as Lars and Catherine had, but with a legal spin.

Back in Washington, we met up with Brandi Graham. She was a woman in her 50s who worked out of Capitol Hill and was the NRA's liaison person. She discussed more campaign marketing with us, so that we could get a perspective of the differences between the NRA and lobbyist groups—what they did and how they operated.

Brandi covered a range of other marketing strategies that had obtained great results, including 'phone messaging pointing', which was easy and inexpensive; and their favourite go-to strategy, 'the $5 campaign'. In a nutshell, this was where you invited a member to donate to the party, offered them a job such as phoning people and encouraged them to be part of the workings of the party, so they felt included. Brandi suggested we speak to different groups and organisations, to lobby them for our cause—gaining support for cheaper energy and the building of dams. This aligned with our One Nation policies and I was keen to learn more about how we could deliver real outcomes through these potential relationships.

It had been a big day, particularly after the night before. I was exhausted and needed to get some sleep. This whirlwind trip was beginning to catch up with me and I was starting to realise that I could no longer keep pace with my younger self. I was burning the candle at both ends, and I missed my wife and home.

Rodger's driver dropped us back at the hotel around 5:30pm. I ate a toasted sandwich, before heading up to my room to shower and to give Deb a call, before heading to bed.

Chapter 28

Big hitters and big business

I woke up and called Deb, before meeting up with James and heading out to get something to eat. Everything was hellishly expensive in the USA, but we found a place that offered a hearty breakfast of steak, eggs and toast for $12.50. This was a bargain considering the size of the meal.

After breakfast, we went for a walk to get our bearings and were astounded at how many electric bikes and scooters there were. People were riding them everywhere and I thought it was a great idea that could be introduced into city centres in Australia, to reduce road congestion.

Being in Washington was quite surreal. It was all so familiar yet strange at the same time. James and I checked out the local area and did all the tourist things. He wanted to go to Macy's to pick up some gifts for his family and I was also keen to check out the famous department store and see if they had anything for Deb and the boys.

We headed back to the Hyatt in time to shower and change for the lunchtime function that Rodger had originally organised for Pauline to attend and speak at. Now we were going in her place, with Rodger and Diana, and James would be delivering Pauline's speech.

The Congressional Sportsmen's Foundation (CSF) was holding the function to discuss the policy priorities for outdoor recreation including hunting, fishing and wildlife conservation.

The function room at the Hyatt Regency on Capitol Hill was full of big hitters from both sides of politics. The delegates included a senator, congressmen, business leaders and ambassadors, such as Dan Harrison and Lucas Hoge, who were both CSF ambassadors.

CSF co-chairs, Senators Jim Risch (a Republican) and Joe Manchin (a Democrat), led the event showing that sportsmen's interests are bipartisan—different political parties were working together towards common goals.

The function ran overtime and James didn't get to speak, which was incredibly disappointing, because it was one of the main reasons we were there—to talk about Australia and how One Nation wanted to make a difference. Pauline's speech covered how we wanted to drought-proof Australia, by building a hybrid of the Bradfield Scheme and more coal-fired power stations. She had also wanted to cover One Nation's firearms' policies and how they would protect the existing rights and laws concerning firearms ownership.

So, instead of making the speech, we tried to network with as many delegates as possible after the function, to share our vision for Australia. I met the State Secretary for Agriculture, Sonny Perdue. I told him we were from Australia and that we had similar problems regarding our environment and protecting it for the future.

I gave him my lucky Donald Trump dollar note that a friend had given me after she'd travelled to Washington, D.C., just before the last US election. I asked him if he would get the president to sign it for me. He said he'd be happy to and would send it to me in Australia.

After the function, I went to freshen up before our next engagement. Rodger had mentioned that Donald Trump was definitely going to be a special guest at the evening function. I was still disappointed that James had not been able to deliver his speech and needed to get my head into a more positive space, before the next engagement.

At 6pm we arrived at the Congressional Sportsmen's Foundation Dinner, where about 1000 people were in attendance, some of whom we'd already met at the lunchtime function. Again, there were congressmen, senators and business people from all over the US.

Before we arrived, Rodger briefed us about what to expect and about American etiquette. He said the best way to gain someone's attention and to hold court on business matters was to have a drink with them. Both James and I definitely could have done with a dry night after the previous night's efforts, but we wanted to ensure we didn't upset anyone. If the Americans loved to have a drink, then we'd have a drink too. And drink they could! We ended up drinking all night and well into the morning.

The night was quite incredible. We mingled for a while, introducing ourselves to as many people as possible. Most were extremely polite and accommodating and some were very passionate about the environment. The event started with the national anthem—everyone stood up at their tables and sang with great patriotism. It was quite a sight to behold and take part in.

The MC went through some housekeeping before the meals began arriving at the tables and the senators and congressmen started their speeches. Their talks were good, with a heavy emphasis on protecting the environment for the generations to come, along with the success of the government and businesses in the US. After the speeches, there was a silent auction with everything on offer from fishing holidays, guided safaris and sporting items of all kinds. Dessert arrived at our table, a delicious cheesecake, which capped off an incredible meal. The Americans sure know how to put on an event.

James and I continued to go around the room, meeting as many people as we could, to make the most of the networking opportunity. We met some incredibly influential people, including Senator Ted Bud whom James managed to line up for the only meeting we would have that wasn't arranged by Rodger.

We met all sorts of fantastic people; such as, Lance, an oil and gas company owner and member of the Dallas Safari Club. His real passion was the conservation of endangered species. We met a woman called Nita, who was an avid shooter and who made environmentally focussed documentaries.

We also met another woman, whose family owned one of the biggest bullet manufacturers in the country; a young Texan bloke, who had just recovered from cancer, who wore the stereotypical ten-gallon hat and who was running for election; and another gentleman who had inherited a bourbon distillery, and who shouted me drinks for much of the night.

By midnight, it was clear Trump wasn't going to show. I now know, from all the conversations I've since had, that he was never going to be there. I didn't know at the time, but it was just another bullshit line that Rodger spun us, as part of story that he wanted to sell.

The Yanks couldn't believe that two Aussies could keep up with them; I didn't know how we could either! Rodger stayed with us most of the night, but he disappeared around 1am. By 3am James and I were well and truly done, and were among the five left, the other being three of the American delegates. We headed back to the hotel, stopping at McDonald's on the way back, for something to eat.

After such a huge day and night, I was absolutely spent and got up very late the next day; it must have been around midday. I didn't even get to speak to Deb, to say good morning, as by the time I woke up, it was 2am back home. Rodger had asked me to send him all the contacts I'd made the previous evening, so I took photos of all the business cards I had collected and texted them to him, before having a shower and heading out.

I came across a man shining shoes, which took me back to my shoe shop days. I sat down and chatted to him while he gave my shoes a first-class polish. He was a lovely down-to-earth gentleman, who did a great job. It was worth every cent of the USD15 I paid.

The first meeting Rodger had lined up for us, that day, was at the National Shooting Sports Foundation. We met a man by the name of Patrick Rothwell who spoke with us about the growth of sporting shooters in the United States and the challenges they were facing within their own country. He spoke about how the second amendment was part of the American Constitution; the Americans are very protective of their rights!

Our next meeting was with Catherine Haggett, the Director of Federal Affairs for Koch Industries—the second largest private company in America, which is involved in everything from building to food production. They were a big deal in the USA. We covered a lot of ground with her, discussing our aim of drought-proofing Australia. We asked whether a company like Koch Industries would come to Australia to build a hybrid of the Bradfield Scheme. We also spoke about building pipelines in Australia, to move gas from WA to QLD.

The issue of drought in Australia was very close to my heart as my family had been forced off their land because of drought, I knew how tough it was for farmers and their families to make ends meet, let alone make a quid on the land, in the best of times. Drought challenges made it even tougher.

Catherine said the company was open to looking at many projects, but obviously she couldn't commit to anything. I told her how building the hybrid of the Bradfield Scheme would open up outback Australia. It would provide agriculture opportunities, cities could be built, forests grown, rivers created and dams built. Potentially, it could create a haven for some endangered species from around the world; the opportunities were almost endless.

After meeting with Catherine, we did some more sightseeing. We hadn't eaten lunch and were starving as it was getting near to dinnertime. Rodger stopped at a food place called Hill Country Barbecue Market that specialised in ribs, beef, ham and pork. The chefs cut up large portions. It was impressive and delicious. I'd never seen anything like it and would definitely put it on my 'to eat again' list.

It was another big day and I was looking forward to calling it a night—the big night before had caught up with me and I couldn't wait to get back to the hotel, to call Deb to tell her I loved her, and to sleep. I'd never been so happy to hit the hay. I turned in at 7pm and didn't move an inch until my phone woke me at the ungodly hour of 2am.

Chapter 29

The set up

The 2am text was James asking if I wanted to get up and shoot some videos at the Lincoln Memorial. At 2:30am, while Washington, D.C. slept, we walked the empty streets. It was still and quiet and it felt as if we had the entire city to ourselves.

We followed a Google map on my phone, looking every bit the tourists, with James pulling his big camera bag on wheels and me carrying his tripod. Passing the White House at that time of the morning was incredible. I could just imagine the President of the United States in there, fast asleep. As we walked, we noticed the secret service observing our every move.

I joked to James, "If there's a sniper on the roof, who thinks we're up to no good, they'll shoot you first with that big bag—it looks as if you're dragging around a bomb!" Mind you, from afar I could have been mistaken for carrying a rifle instead of a tripod, so I wouldn't have been far behind him.

I don't know if curiosity got the better of the secret service, seeing two blokes walking along in the dead hours of the morning, or whether they pulled everyone up, but it wasn't long before a couple of them approached us to ask what we were doing and where were we going. When two guys with guns ask you questions, you answer them—quickly! We said we were headed to the Lincoln Memorial to do some filming and showed them the camera.

They were friendly enough, giving us directions, but solidly within their roles as protectors of the president and his family.

We arrived at the deserted memorial about 3 am and set up the video equipment. As we stood in such a significant place, it was hard not to get lost in thoughts about all the people who had been there before us: Martin Luther King, JFK, all the people protesting the Vietnam War, and so many others.

We began shooting the video for the Facebook page, and I spoke about democracy and how important it is, not only here in the United States but also back home in Australia. We got about halfway in, when a security officer spotted us and came over. She said, "You can't do that here". We explained what we were doing and she said, "All good, but hurry it up, and then move on Sirs".

After we finished at the Lincoln Memorial, we walked over to the Korean War Memorial and the Vietnam War Memorial. As the heat of the day began sifting into the cooler early morning temperature, I could almost imagine being in Vietnam. The statues looked real as the shifting morning shadows animated them and made them look as if they were moving in front of your eyes.

We walked back to the hotel with the tall, white, pointed Washington Monument looming over us, standing guard and keeping us in its sights until we got to the entrance of the hotel and out of view. By 4:30am, our early morning adventure was over and I went back to bed to get some more sleep before the day began—again.

The first meeting of the day at a very civilised 11am and was one James had set up with Senator Ted Bud.

We discussed a number of things with him for about an hour and he spoke about his concerns around the Middle East.

The Australian government was looking at spending up to $220 billion on French-made diesel electric submarines—a contract that wouldn't be delivered until the middle of the 2030s. I believed Australia needed better defences, now, to protect the Australian people and our way of life. Australia could buy six new nuclear submarines for $3.6 billion each in the USA. I suggested to the senator that it would be a great idea for his government to contact their counterparts in the Australian government, about the possibility of our leasing or buying these from the States.

I also discussed how many Australian politicians and parties were 'in bed' with the Chinese government or were taking political donations from Chinese businesses. We only have one country, and I feel strongly about keeping its interests safe for our future generations. It was a great conversation. He was good to speak to and keen to build better relations with Australia and its people.

Rodger and his driver picked us up from Senator Budd's office, near Capitol Hill, and we drove around for a while seeing more of the sights, before going to a packed, old-fashioned sports bar that had TVs all over the walls, and which were playing everything from basketball to racing, hockey and gridiron. Diana met us there.

Rodger bought James and I a drink called a Bourbon Fireball, it sounded lethal and it was the longest drink I've ever waited for—it took at least an hour for it to arrive! I don't know what was in it, but it tasted like death. Not wanting to be rude or to offend, James and I had a crack at it.

Within a few sips, James felt so crook that Rodger called his driver to take him back to the hotel. I managed to drink a quarter of it before I just couldn't take another sip without gaging—it was bloody shocking. I had to give up on it.

We'd been at the sports bar for a couple of hours, before Diana left to go home. I said to Rodger that I was keen to head back to the hotel and check up on James. Really though, I was done with drinking. Geez they could drink! I knew I was beyond drunk, but at the same time, I was aware of a weird sensation like a huge constant rush of adrenalin that had been racing through my system since drinking the Fireball. I'd never felt like this from alcohol before. I wondered if there was something in my drink that wasn't supposed to be there or if I was allergic to something. I didn't know. All I knew was I didn't feel right—something was wrong.

Looking back at the pictures that were taken of me at the bar, my eyes look crazy and wired. When Deb and I looked at the photos, back in Australia, she asked what was with my eyes. Deb and I had the odd Scotch here or there, but we weren't big drinkers and in our 34 years together, she's only seen me truly drunk maybe five or six times. I had never before looked or felt the way I did that night, nor have I since.

Rodger's driver picked us up from the bar and we were heading back to my hotel when Rodger asked would I come to a local strip club with him. Pissed as a nit and buzzing, I stupidly said, "Ok, when in Rome!" What I *should* have said was a big, "Hell no!" I *should* have used my brain, listened to my gut and called it a night. Unfortunately I didn't.

The last time I had been a strip club was in my late teens, with a few of my best mates in Brisbane. On that occasion, we weren't there long before a huge fight erupted and everyone was thrown out onto the curb—it was a madhouse!

Back in Washington, I vaguely recall pulling up outside a narrow building. Rodger and an African American guy led me inside through a large crowd of people. I then had to navigate my way up some stairs. Inside the club, there were people everywhere and I was taken to a seat close to the dance pole, where I gratefully sat down.

Rodger ordered more scotches, as the dancer swung around on the pole. I ordered a steak sandwich, in an attempt to sober up a bit, which was futile because Rodger just kept the drinks coming. I was going downhill fast.

One of the strippers motioned for me to come forward, as Rodger handed me a bundle of US notes. He shoved me, whilst egging me on. I stood up and staggered forward a few steps intending to give her the money, but she threw one of her legs onto my shoulder. I don't remember how long I stood there, but I remember being thankful for being able to make it back to the table, where I half-slid, and half-fell back into my seat.

Rodger pulled out another wad of notes and a woman appeared and began to proposition me. Rodger asked what she was saying. "She's asking if she can give me a blow job", I raved like some disgusting eighteen-year-old idiot, showing off in front of Rodger and saying the most stupid things.

The dumbest thing I've ever done in all my 57 years was go to that strip club!

I got up from my seat and stumbled to the toilet. I was finding it really difficult to walk properly and I vaguely remember thinking, "How the hell do I get out of here?" Back at the table, I told Rodger, "It's time to go". His driver picked us up and took me back to the hotel, where I gratefully fell onto my bed and slept.

When I woke up the next morning, I was still fully dressed in my clothes from the night before.

As the night's happenings came back to me. I recalled being at the strip club and felt incredibly silly. I tried to justify my stupidity, "Thousands of Aussie blokes have done the same thing". Foolish? Absolutely! But, not condemning. I thought back to Kevin Rudd's having gone to a strip club in New York, some ten years earlier.

I should have known better. If I had been Joe Blow, it wouldn't have been a thing. I called Deb and told her I'd been to a strip club. She laughed and said, "I've been to a couple of hen's nights where there were strippers!" We had a good laugh as I told her what little I could remember of the night.

Chapter 30

Home sweet home

After my call to Deb, James and I hired a couple of electric bikes and rode around Washington, visiting the Thomas Jefferson Memorial, the National Museum of Natural History, the White House and a number of other landmarks. We returned the bikes after lunch, and Rodger and his driver picked us up and drove us back to Virginia, to a major shopping centre where James was keen to pick up some more gifts.

The mall was an absolute hive of activity—the US economy was on fire. I went inside for a while, but was feeling unwell, so I told James and Rodger that I would go and wait for them in the car. I think I was just really tired—all the drinking, the different food, and the really late

nights had caught up with me. I was used to getting up at 4am and going to bed by 10pm. Exhausted, I laid the seat back and slept for a couple of hours in the warm car.

When they arrived back, Rodger asked us where we wanted to go next. I wanted to buy some cigars for Paul, a good friend of mine who loved them. He took us to a place called Cigar World and I picked up four cigars that were about 200mm long and thick as a 20-cent piece. They were so cheap in comparison to Australian prices.

On the way back to Washington, D.C., we visited Arlington Cemetery. Being there and thinking about all the people who gave their lives for their country was a poignant experience. I was almost moved to tears, as I reflected on how many Australians have given their lives for our freedom.

Rodger said he needed to stop at a firearms' shop on the way back to the hotel. I was keen to see inside an American firearms' store. We pulled up and went into a Nova Armory, which sold all kinds of handguns and long arms. It was very different from our gun shops; you couldn't buy most of the stuff in this store in Australia, for example the kinds of weapon that our military and police had. However, in the US it was all on show and available to buy over the counter. It was quite impressive.

By the time we got back to the hotel, it was 7pm. I got something to eat from Starbucks and headed straight to bed. I was looking forward to catching the plane home the next day.

My last few hours on American soil were spent waking at 7:30am, followed by a quick call to Deb, steak and eggs for breakfast, a short stroll with James to buy a few last minute gifts, packing up and checking out around lunchtime.

Rodger drove us to the airport, where we said our goodbyes and thanked him for his hospitality before boarding the flight from

Washington, D.C. to Los Angeles. This would be the last time I would lay eyes on Rodger Muller in person. The flight home seemed much longer. It was almost six hours to LA, followed by the fifteen-hour economy class flight to Sydney. I slept as much as I could on the plane, so I could be refreshed when I got home, but at 183cms tall, it was pretty tight and cramped. I ended up dozing between movies to pass the time and to keep my mind off the discomfort.

After landing in Sydney, we headed to the domestic gate for our connecting flight to Brisbane. I was absolutely chomping at the bit to get back home and to see Deb, but I got a lesson in patience instead, as we missed the flight because of a delay at customs and Sydney's notorious peak-hour traffic. James and I killed some more time in the Virgin Lounge discussing our trip. We both agreed it had been a productive journey and one we had enjoyed.

However, with nearly 30 hours of travelling time, all the alcohol and food, it was a bit too much for me. I doubted I'd do it again in a hurry—I was exhausted, but eager to get back to work and to put some of what I'd learn in the US into place. We finally arrived in Brisbane, and shared a cab back to James' place where I picked up my car and headed home.

Travelling is a fantastic experience, but there's never any place quite like home. Arriving home to Deb was better than anything else. I'd missed her so much. She looked as exhausted as I did, from having to look after the house and two-and-a-half acres of garden, as well as everything else while I was away.

Deb had got so much done in the time I was gone—the latest renos and the crafts she'd done while I was away were a great credit to her. Christmas was coming up and she had made a number of her amazing personalised Christmas trees. She makes these for people who have touched her heart in some way throughout the year—they looked fantastic.

We chatted while we unpacked my bag, and talked about was happening at home and with our boys; Christian, who lived on the Sunshine Coast; and Zeik, who lived in Brisbane. Both were busy working.

By the time Deb had thrown on a load of washing, I had well and truly hit the wall and went for a kip, but ended up sleeping right through until the following morning.

I had a couple of days' rest, catching up with everyone at home, before ploughing back into work, meeting up with Pauline, connecting with all the candidates, getting our policies through and preparing for elections.

We were just nine months out from the 2019 federal election and the campaign was in full swing. It was all hands on deck as we did interviews, designed and printed out signs and put up billboards across the country. We attended functions and meetings and filmed footage for our social media pages.

We were aiming to secure at least one seat in every state, and possibly two in Queensland. It was looking as we would succeed. If we did, it would mean that One Nation gained the balance of power in the upper house and we would possibly be able to achieve our aims.

Malcolm Roberts and I travelled up and down the east coast of QLD with James Ashby, stopping at all the towns and cities on the way to ensure we were across all their challenges and that we understood what it was that the public wanted and needed. We had meetings with farmers, fishermen, trucking companies, educators, businesses, retirees and youth workers; you name it met them.

I agreed with all of One Nation's policies, but for me the ones that I was the most passionate about getting across the line—for my family and the future—were ensuring the security of our country in terms of land/utility ownership and immigration, along with the cost of delivery of water and energy. I believed One Nation had a lot of potential. Pauline Hanson is as honest as they come. She's passionate and patriotic with a determined desire to make Australia a better place to live in.

Anyone who's spent any length of time with Pauline will tell you she is one of the least racist people you'll ever meet. The media love portraying her as a racist, but that's far from the truth. They love to hate her and when you look back on past interviews, you'll see she made a lot of sense and a great deal of what she predicted has come to pass.

As a senator, I hoped to be instrumental in bringing people together, to create more jobs and opportunities for Australians with new and improved plans for agriculture, manufacturing, defence and infrastructure.

Chapter 31

Al Jazeera

The election was announced on April the 11th 2019. Thirty-five days before that, on the 7th of March, I received an email from a group called the Al Jazeera Network, who listed their address on the letterhead as Doha, Qatar, in the Middle East. I had no clue who they were, but I opened it up and began to read...

"Al Jazeera's Investigative Unit is in the final stages of preparing two documentaries concerning the pro-gun lobby in the United States and its interactions with Pauline Hanson's One Nation party in Australia.

The Investigative Unit is part of Al Jazeera Media Network, an international television network, which broadcasts its programs around the world.

As part of our research for these programs, an undercover investigator infiltrated parts of the U.S. gun lobby and, over a three-year period, observed their activities.

Undercover investigators also observed the activities of Pauline Hanson's One Nation party in Australia as members of the party prepared for meetings with officials from the U.S. gun lobby and also as representatives of Pauline Hanson's One Nation party visited the United States and attended a series of meetings with members of the U.S. gun lobby in Washington, D.C. and in Fairfax, Virginia.

We are aware that, as the leader of the Queensland branch of Pauline Hanson's One Nation party and a candidate for the Senate in the upcoming federal elections in Australia, you were involved in meetings described above.

It is our intention to broadcast details of these activities, including comments made by you, in our two scheduled programs in March, 2019."

The Al Jazeera Network added they wanted a written response by 18:00 AEDT on March the 20th 2019.

Al Jazeera? Who the hell were they? I thought it had to be some kind of joke at first, similar to those Nigerian money extortionists. The whole thing didn't seem legit and if they hadn't referenced One Nation in the letter, I probably would have tossed it in the bin and not given it another thought.

I wasn't sure who these people were, but I thought I'd better check them out just to be sure. I typed their name into a Google search, not expecting to see anything. I was a bit stunned when the search came up with pages and pages of information, all confirming that Al Jazeera is a privately-owned media network in the Middle East.

A further search revealed the Qatari government funded them. I just couldn't understand it. What would a Middle Eastern company want with Australian politics or me for that matter? It just didn't make any sense.

I reread the letter and its mention of meetings with the gun lobby. I thought about Rodger Muller—he'd *have* to know something about this for sure.

Rodger had been in contact with Pauline and James earlier in the year and had met up with them at a restaurant called Megalomania Yeppon, to ask Pauline to do a video for him. As with me, he had plied them with alcohol and had tried to set Pauline up with leading questions about the Port Arthur Massacre. You should never underestimate Pauline; she's one clever woman and she wasn't having a bar of his crap and didn't buy into his agenda at all. It was another great example of Rodger's behind the scenes skulduggery.

I hadn't seen Rodger, since the US trip, but I had spoken to him a few times, although we mostly communicated via text message. The last time I'd heard from him was on the 18th of February 2019, when I texted him to call me about Castle Law in the UK. He had mentioned it previously, and I was after some more information on it. He messaged me back saying, "Hey Steve, I'm a little caught up at the moment and travelling, I'll call you asap", but he never did. Now I know why—the rotten mongrel bastard!

The first call I made, after receiving the letter, was to James Ashby, who in turn called Pauline and the three of us discussed the email. It turned out that they would receive the same email the following day.

None of us had ever dealt with Al Jazeera and we couldn't work out if they were for real, or it was just a whole lot of spin from them, or maybe from someone pretending to be them? We really didn't have any idea. Pauline said the best thing to do was to hand it to a lawyer who could get to the bottom of it, and report it to the Australian Federal Police and ASIO, who could do a follow up investigation as well.

What we did figure out was that Rodger was definitely a part of it, as he had set up all the meetings they mentioned; so, we called him. It was no surprise when he didn't answer. I left a message and sent a follow up text, "Rodger could you please give me a call, thanks mate, Steve". In fact, everything associated with Rodger Muller and Gun Rights' Australia was gone—his email, his website, the Facebook page had all disappeared. It got stranger by the day.

Al Jazeera's deadline to respond to them came and went, as we ignored their threat. We were confident of not having done anything wrong and therefore didn't buy into whatever accusation, conspiracy theory or other garbage they were spinning. It was clear to us that whatever they claimed was fabricated, and a ploy to bring down One Nation; but why?

We found out that the two-part documentary was due to air on the ABC, on the 25th and 27th of March, just two days after the NSW election. Apparently, the ABC had purchased the documentary, which was in the final stages of editing, from Al Jazeera for $5000 in-kind.

We put Al Jazeera to the back of our minds, and got on with the job at hand, which was the NSW election on March the 23rd, as well as the federal election that was being held on May the 18th. Malcom Roberts, from Brisbane, was number one on the senate ticket and I was number two. We were a team.

Malcolm was a great bloke, short in stature but large in life experience, strength and guts. A quietly spoken man, he meditated every morning and was very balanced and calm; however, he never once ran away from a fight. Highly intelligent, he'd listen to any good argument and make up his own mind about where he sat on the issue. I respected him and his opinion.

Our first stop on the campaign trail was Gympie, where we met with the local One Nation members, for a barbecue on Sunday March the 10th.

Malcolm and I spoke about policies and answered questions that the local branch members had about current issues. Everybody was in high spirits.

On March the 11th, James and I had a phone conference with Mark Latham. We had to let him know that something was going to hit the media, from a group called Al Jazeera, and none of us knew exactly what it was. It would be an understatement to say that Mark took it well, when we told him that the letters we had received indicated some kind of damaging undertone, regarding One Nation and the NRA, and that possibly Rodger Muller was behind it. Even though we hadn't done a thing wrong, we all hoped the story wouldn't come out until after the NSW election, so there was nothing to side track anyone.

It was a busy time and all our schedules were full to the brim. I'd been doing interviews with Paul Murray Live, the Peter Gleeson show, radio interviews, and a heap of other daily meetings.

Our next stop was Townsville, where Malcolm and I inspected washed out bridges and other high priority issues that needed attention. Townsville's was challenged by their youth running wild which was of great concern and something we needed to get on to. We hoped we'd win the election so we could engage Geoff and Vicky Toomby, who had a large property where they catered for the rehabilitation of young people. Vicky taught them to cook and look after themselves, working on their self-esteem and Geoff taught them how to muster, ride and work on the land.

Most people don't know that it costs the taxpayer $547,500 per child, per year, ($1,500 per day) to house a young person in juvenile detention. Geoff and Vicki were rehabilitating them by teaching them important life skills for less than $50K. It was a no-brainer; why the government didn't see that, who knew!

By March the 19th, I was back in Brisbane doing more media and talking about a range of policies. One issue I raised was concerned why Prime Minister Scott Morrison's preferences were going to the ALP ahead of One Nation. As usual, One Nation was a headache for the major parties, and they just weren't prepared to let Pauline or One Nation get a foothold in federal politics—they were scared. Pauline and One Nation kept them honest and they didn't like to be held accountable.

On March the 22nd, I headed down to Tweed Heads on the QLD/NSW border to attend a three-day medical cannabis forum. People were there from all over the world, including Olivia Newton John's husband, John Easterling, who is a big supporter of the use of medical cannabis. Lucy Haslam was also there. Her fight to legalise medical marijuana is deeply personal, as her son Daniel was diagnosed with stage-four bowel cancer at the age of twenty, and only found relief from his nausea by taking medicinal cannabis. The leader of the Greens, Richard Di Natale, was there too; we didn't agree on everything, but we agreed on medicinal cannabis.

The building was packed with supporters, suppliers, growers and importers, showcasing medicinal cannabis, textiles, food derivatives, and other products and all stressing that it will be big business in the near future.

Australia should take full advantage of this new and upcoming business opportunity, but they won't, because of their obligations under the United Nations' Convention (single convention on narcotic drugs, 1961). The truth is that opium-based drugs kill 41 people a day in the United States, on average, (according to 2018 data). However, medicinal cannabis has not killed anybody. Australia currently grows 50% of the world's raw medical opium supplies.

If our politicians told the UN to bugger off, and led instead of following, then our country would be a leading world supplier of medicinal cannabis to the Australian and overseas markets.

Election day came in NSW and I wished Mark Latham all the best, to which he responded, "Thanks very much". I sat around the TV that evening, watching the votes coming in and was thrilled when Mark Latham and Rod Roberts, who was number two on the ticket, were both in a strong position. A few weeks later, it became apparent that both had won an upper house spot each, which was fantastic. Things were going well for One Nation—we were headed in the right direction.

Chapter 32

The smear campaign

Malcolm Roberts and I wanted to go after Rodger Muller and Al Jazeera. Neither of us could work out what the hell their motive was, but Pauline said, "No, let's just wait and see what it's all about". The lawyer had sent a letter off to the AFP and ASIO, so we played the waiting game, but not for long.

Back home, on March the 25th, I sat down in the lounge, with Deb and our eldest son, Christian, to watch the first episode of the Al Jazeera produced, *How to Sell a Massacre*. As it played, we watched in both horror and disbelief as Peter Charley, a journalist from Al Jazeera whom I'd never heard of, portrayed me as some gun nut and racist who was trying to extract millions of dollars from the NRA and Koch Industries to set up branch of the NRA in Australia.

The documentary showed us listening to the NRA representatives talking about how they market, with Peter Charley's commentary over the top of most of it to make it look as if we agreed with everything they were saying.

It got worse as it went on. It had me saying that I would change the national gun laws and entertain shooters from America in Parliament House; that I would start charging shooters to come to Australia for trips, to shoot feral pigs, deer, and horses, all the while showing me looking at firearms, as it was some kind of gun pornography.

The hypothetical conversation that Rodger led in the USA, asking us what money we would really need to win seats, was taken completely out of context and cut and re-pieced together with Peter Charley's commentary, to lead the viewer into a false perception. All we did was answer what was clearly a set up/planned question.

Rodger, the undercover agent or journalist, asked us how much we would need, realistically, to achieve the balance of power. However, Peter Charley's narrative completely manipulated the viewer into believing we were talking about it as if we were actually going to ask the NRA for money, which was a complete fabrication.

James didn't escape their sights either. He was portrayed in a similar manner to me. We were gobsmacked. Not only had these mongrels secretly filmed me at every meeting, luncheon and event, while we were in the USA but the way they edited it with Peter's commentary made everything appear different from the reality of the situation. It was a complete smear campaign of me, of James and of the One Nation party, with a focus on us asking for money and One Nation 'softening' gun laws to be in line with the NRA's perspective. It was all bullshit!

I discussed the rot we were seeing on national TV with both Pauline and James and we decided enough was enough. We agreed James and I would front the media, back in Brisbane, the following afternoon and respond to the lies and ridiculous accusations these lunatics had made.

By the time daylight broke, the media pack was already outside our house. Deb couldn't believe it and neither could I. Just after midday, I gave her a kiss and she wished me good luck as I grabbed my things and headed for my car. As I drove out through our gate, the media launched forward with one guy shoving a camera right into the car through my partially-open window. Journalists yelled questions at me and got angry, when I waved them off.

As the media engulfed the car, I had to come to a complete stop and I asked the guy to get his camera out of my window. I told them I was heading to Brisbane and that both James and I would front the media there and answer any questions they had. For some reason that wasn't good enough for them and, in the end, I had to ask them politely to move away from the vehicle, so that no one would get hurt as I drove away.

I did end up doing an interview on my way to Brisbane. Steve Austin called me from ABC Radio. He's always been a reasonable fellow, so I accepted his request to interview me over the phone. It was good preparation for what was to come.

James and I fronted the media outside the Sky News headquarters. We were grilled by the media for an exhaustive 39 minutes, all of which, which was broadcast live and nationwide. We responded to everything they threw at us and we made it perfectly clear that the documentary was completely manipulated. We explained that everything had been filmed secretly and pieced together to make a fabricated show. The media didn't really care. They loved the fact that there was yet another controversial story about Pauline that they could run with. I think we made our point, but they had already made their minds up—One Nation would never get a fair go against the ABC and Al Jazeera.

In the second part of *How to Sell a Massacre*, Pauline was made to look foolish, and they tried to use the Port Arthur shootings to frame her as a conspiracy nut. Similar to their portrayal of James and I, their depiction of Pauline was nothing short of fiction, as they went on about gun laws and the NRA. For a while, it looked as if Al Jazeera had achieved their mission of trying to destroy Pauline and One Nation, and me along with them.

On March the 28th, Pauline, James and I held a media conference where Pauline read out a statement that we had prepared collectively.

Pauline presented it and she was pretty upset with the media in general.

"Today is a day of shame on the Australian media who have been sold a story that is too good to be true and you took it hook, line and sinker. Media across Australia have been blinded by their hate and bias towards One Nation and myself, and rushed to report on the heavily edited footage. These covert recordings have never been seen in full and the footage has been heavily edited. Therefore, comments aired have been taken completely out of context.

Admissions have been made by the Qatar government funded organisation Al Jazeera - that myself and One Nation had zero affiliation or connection with the NRA.

When Al Jazeera discovered this, they orchestrated meetings with the National Rifle Association and donors to the American president Donald Trumps election campaign.

Let me make it very clear to the Australian people - **I have never sought donations or policy guidance from the NRA**. An approach by Rodger Muller who was working undercover for the Islamic organisation, made an offer to me to be a guest speaker at the annual Congressional Sportsman dinner in September 2018."

The media conference ran for roughly eighteen minutes. After it was over, we left the room without taking any further questions. Public opinion was divided; we would just have to wait and see what Australians thought of our response, or should I say Pauline's response.

Chapter 33

The con

I've made a few mistakes in my life, but allowing Rodger Muller and his accomplices into my life—into my home, to meet my wife and eat at our table—was by far the biggest mistake. How could I have recognised him to be a Middle Eastern undercover agent, looking to undermine the entire fabric of my existence! It was like something out of a movie. These kinds of things just didn't happen to everyday people—especially not to a country boy from rural Queensland.

I was only just becoming aware of the sheer magnitude of what was happening. A thousand questions accompanied these soul-searching internal thoughts. I just could not understand why a media outlet, which was owned and controlled by the Qatari royal family and government, would want anything to do with Pauline, James, and me; or with One Nation for that matter! What did they have to gain? Why did they desperately want to bring us down; and why on earth did they spend three years planning it?

In the days that followed, Peter Charley told a reporter on the ABC that he had set the whole thing up. He had hired his 'old mate' Rodger Muller on behalf of Al Jazeera, adding that he was the best man for the job. It was hardly surprising when you watched how Peter had completely manipulated the footage and his story to suit his smear campaign. But, still the question remained: why? Why was this guy so hell bent on inventing such a story? What was his beef with One Nation?

The thing that perplexed me the most was that the only party who had actually promised to soften gun laws was the Tasmanian Liberal government.

So why go after One Nation? I exhausted my own thinking desperately trying to come up with a logical reason why we were the primary targets.

Rodger Muller, Peter Charley and Diana Armatta—all Al Jazeera employees—had set One Nation up for a fall, right from the get-go. Whom were they ultimately working for?

Rodger's part in it now became clearer to me, as an Aussie who portrayed himself and his organisation Gun Rights Australia as the protectors of our existing gun rights. Talking up and big noting himself about his experiences at the Lindt Café in Sydney, his trips to the USA, and his meetings with Donald Trump Jr., senators and congressmen—these were all 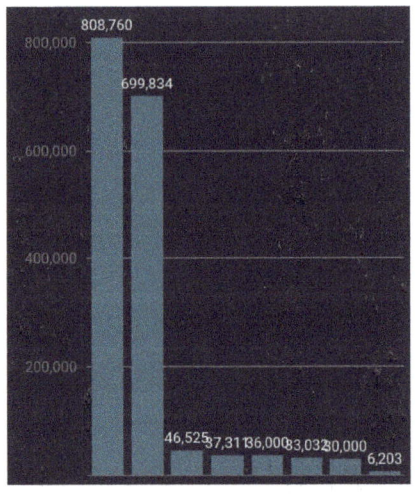 fabricated stories he told to build a character that he pulled from his own fiction novel. As we began to join the dots, we wondered whether his real name was even Rodger Muller—who knew! What we did know was he was nothing more than an undercover agent for a foreign media outlet. He was paid to target One Nation and bring it to its knees . . . and I was just a pawn in the game.

Then, we then discovered that 'Diana Armatta's real name was Claudianna Blanco, and that she was a journalist who worked for SBS radio, with a Masters in documentary filmmaking. The web become more intricate as the characters revealed themselves for who they really were.

On the face of it, Rodger Muller could have been Australia's greatest conman, given the long line of people he successfully lied to and manipulated. They included me, James, Pauline, the NRA, Koch Industries, senators, congressmen, customs, the Department of Home Affairs, the US Department of Homeland Security, and even Donald Trump Jr., if indeed he did know him—my God!

As the accusations that were thrown at James, Pauline, the NRA, Koch Industries and myself, came from pieces of footage that had been shot over a number of years, as well as my small part in the documentary, and were easy to explain. Rodger got James and I on the grog, knowing in advance what footage he wanted. He deliberately asked certain questions while we were drunk, and then cut and paste bits of audio and footage together to make it look like a damning story, when it actually wasn't.

Comments that were aired, such as, "Muslims are breaking into houses and stealing everything" were taken completely out of context and set in to make it look as if I was a racist and hated Muslims, which is far from the truth. One Nation had a Muslim candidate, Emma Eros, in the NSW election! The way they twisted my words was extraordinary!

More accusations against James, Pauline and me rolled out, including one that I wanted to weaken the gun laws in Australia—totally untrue. They portrayed me as a person, who supported massacres in the USA—also lies and fabrications. Al Jazeera had a plan. None of this happened by accident, and it must have cost them a small fortune to focus on this for more than three years; paying their people and footing the bill for all the travel they did.

A contact in the media industry later informed me that this sting would have cost millions. It seems like a lot of money, to bring down an Australian political party.

They paid Australian, American and Argentinian agents to arrange every meeting that took place in the United States, and they set up and filmed every step of our entire trip, as well as what they filmed here on Australian soil. They secretly videoed and tape-recorded in my own home, in NSW, and in Pauline's federal parliamentary office—knowing full well that they were breaking every ethical code in the Media, Entertainment and Arts Alliance (MEAA) book. Even if they had portrayed us in a positive light, it would still have been unethical. Every journalist in the country is meant to disclose that they are a journalist, working for an organisation, and Rodger Muller clearly did not do this.

Every media outlet in the world swallowed this story without checking any of the so-called facts. Not one of the characters in their two-part documentary was contacted for a right of reply. Not one bit was fact checked—the media just ran with it, republishing and replaying the fabricated story.

The slander was as appalling as it was disappointing. We never once asked the NRA or Koch Industries for money. The footage showed James and I drunk, together with other people who had been drinking into the early hours of the morning, all of us talking as people who've had way too many talk. The bullshit was flying; the fishing stories and the 'mine's bigger than yours' stuff. That was all it was and nothing more.

Al Jazeera and their agents picked out bits and mashed them together to make us look as bad as they could and it *almost* worked. To the Australian public's credit, they saw it for what it was—a total con job. Only the true political hacks used it to their advantage.

The Left called us every despicable name in the book. We even had to weather being called traitors to Australia, which was the most insulting—anyone who knew Pauline, James or me found it laughable and it would have been if the slander weren't so bloody hurtful.

We regrouped and focused on what we had to do.

After a few days without any more fodder, the story got old and just faded away. The mud had been thrown and it had dried out; so the media turned their attention to destroying someone else's life.

It was tough, but the worst was yet to come three weeks later.

Chapter 34

Crushed

The next few weeks were spent helping candidates here on the Sunshine Coast and keeping in touch with candidates throughout the state. Something was always happening—candidates not having enough 'how to vote' cards or wanting advice on how to handle various situations. I spent a lot of time with them at their market days or going to meetings with them—it was a busy time.

Nominations for the federal election closed at midday on April the 23rd. I was now officially on the ballot paper for the election and running for the Australian Senate. My name was directly below Malcolm Roberts, on the paper, and One Nation had drawn the B section, which meant I had second position on the ballot paper.

For the next few days, I was busy organising things for Anzac Day, finalising a Local Government Association Queensland (LGAQ) questionnaire relating to commitments and support for projects throughout QLD. I was also arranging marketing information for Barry—a strong supporter of Pauline Hanson and Tony Abbott, who wanted to put up advertising endorsing them both.

Come Friday, I helped Malcolm Roberts prepare two medicinal cannabis bills, which were to be introduced to parliament after the election, and then I knocked off for the week and headed home to Deb.

I didn't stop much over that weekend. I spent a day catching up on yard work, then travelled around the Sunshine Coast putting corflutes on sticks before we got into the full swing of the election campaign, which was due to begin on Monday.

At 5:30pm on Sunday April the 28th, the phone rang—it was a woman, named Jennifer, calling from a news channel. She told me there was an ad playing on Channel 9, previewing *A Current Affair*'s Monday night episode. It was about a married politician in a secret video and she asked if she could get an interview with me. I didn't understand why she'd want to speak with me about it and I asked her why. That's when she said, "You're in it".

I had no idea what it could be about or what the hell was going on, so I asked her to send a copy through to me so I could take a look and get back to her. Minutes later, the video landed in my inbox and my whole world imploded with it. I was absolutely devastated. I could not believe what I was watching. It was as if all my worst nightmares had been rolled into a one-minute horror movie.

The Al Jazeera agents had done it again. I could barely watch the video, without feeling sick. I just could not believe what I was seeing.

The video showed me behaving drunkenly and foolishly. There was no mistaking the purpose of this video. The Al Jazeera agents were clearly upset that their documentary had not had the desired effect and that One Nation was still strong. They had decided to pull out all the stops, to bring them to their knees and, in this case, it meant using me as a sacrificial lamb. This video would put One Nation in the media spotlight once again, for all the wrong reasons.

I was speechless. I had no idea what to say or do. I felt completely crushed for myself, for Pauline, and for One Nation. However, more than anyone else, I was totally destroyed for Deb and my family.

Fortunately, I had told Deb that I'd been to a strip club with Rodger Muller, but seeing it on the TV, with me acting so disgracefully, like a drunken idiot, wasn't going to be easy on her. I wouldn't have blamed her for kicking me out then and there.

The first thing I did was tell Deb, "Those bastards have done it again!" and then I showed her the video. She'd seen how Al Jazeera had set up One Nation and me in the documentary *How to Sell a Massacre*, and that was probably my saving grace. Watching her watch the video was beyond destroying. I saw how badly it hurt her.

Deb was in total shock. She remained speechless for what seemed like an eternity before she finally said, "I can't believe Rodger and Diana would stoop this low!" She felt as if it was a personal attack on her, and she believed it was their way of trying to destroy our marriage.

The second thing I did was to call James, who dialled Pauline into the conversation. I told them what I knew, which was what the promo had shown and I told them what *ACA* had said about it. Pauline said, "We will just have to wait and see what comes out".

I had not told anybody, but Deb, that I'd been to a strip club in Washington, D.C. and I'm sure both James and Pauline were upset about it—why wouldn't they be, it was an irresponsible thing for me to do. I never should have gotten so drunk that I made such bad decisions. It was out of character and not a true reflection of the person I am.

I had already had a taste of what Al Jazeera could do, and I was nervous about what sort of job they were going to do on this one. The show was only a little over 24 hours away, but time slowed and I couldn't sleep; minutes seemed like hours, and hours seemed like days.

Finally, it was Monday night. Christian came over with his partner to support Deb and me, when the segment aired. If the ad was bad, the whole segment was like watching a train crash—I didn't want to see it but I couldn't look away. I had been totally setup by Rodger Muller . . . again. I had done nothing illegal, but the media didn't care about that; they were in a feeding frenzy. I knew this wouldn't end well and my brain felt as if it was going to explode.

Deb began crying and I just kept apologising over and over. Later she said she was shocked and confused—she had been with me for 32 years and not once had she seen me so intoxicated and so disrespectful towards women. It was truly shocking. My son consoled both of us, saying it was going to be ok. He and his partner were our rock throughout this whole debacle.

Then the phone lit up as the calls, text messages and emails began flooding in. All were incredibly sympathetic and reassuring. Family and friends, politicians, even journalists offered support and left messages such as, "Stay strong, Steve, none of us are without blemishes" and, "You have done so much good and you have been a wonderful husband and father, hang in there". I was lucky to have such amazing people in my life.

Later that evening, after the segment had aired, I spoke with Pauline and James. Pauline was more concerned about Deb than the fallout it had created for the One Nation party. That was Pauline; always putting people first and seeing through the bullshit. She said to me, "Steve, have a think about what you want to do".

Even with all the support and encouragement, I was crushed. I had never felt so broken. My thoughts swirled around the way they had set me up, about my loss of faith in Australian journalism and, most importantly, the damage it had done to my family and my career. What a dirty cut-throat business politics can be.

I couldn't see the media letting go of this, it all felt way beyond me. It had hurt Deb, my family, the party, the candidates, and my electorate—literally everyone.

Chapter 35

The aftermath

That first night was one of many sleepless ones that followed. Deb and I shed many tears and I kept wondering why this was happening. What had we done to deserve such pain?

At about 4am, Deb got up and pulled back the curtains. At first it looked as if it was daylight outside, it was so bright; but then she realised it wasn't the sun beaming into the room, it was all the lights and cameras from the media camped out in front of our driveway—they were everywhere!

There were cars all over the place and journalists were falling over each other to get the best vantage point. Deb yelled, "Steve quick pull all the curtains closed and lock all the windows at the front of the house". Deb ran around the house and locked all of the downstairs windows and doors. She later said she remembers thinking, "Holy shit! Steve hasn't murdered anyone, he hasn't hurt anyone, and he hasn't stolen anything. He's not a paedophile, and he's done nothing wrong. God forbid—he's been to a strip club!"

Our house was like Fort Knox, with everything closed to prevent our home and life being telecast live around the world. Channels 7, 9 and Ten, the ABC, SBS, the Washington Post, The Age, The Australian, AAP, The Guardian, the British Times, Chinese newspapers, and every single radio station known to man—all were vying to get the scoop.

My son phoned to check on us and asked if we needed any support. Deb wanted to say yes, but it would have been impossible for him even to get on the property, with the media circus out the front, so we told him not to come.

I was out of my mind and don't remember much about what happened in those first few days, but Deb clearly remembers our son contacting one of our neighbours to get permission to enter our property through his. He brought milk and bread and other supplies with him and managed to sneak in before the media shit storm fully erupted. The media morphed into something Deb had never witnessed before. She watched our house, and the strip club video, going viral on every TV and media outlet worldwide. "For God sake he's been to a strip club!" she kept saying.

She told me there was one moment, when she was lying on the bed watching the media's take on the video, and she thought, "You bastard Rodger, you bastard!" She had much the same to say about Diana.

The more global it went, the more I regressed, to the point where Deb found me curled up in a foetal position, broken. My phone didn't stop with calls, messages and requests from journalists at our front gate asking me to 'come out and talk to us'. They constantly hounded us, to get their piece of flesh.

The media justified their harassment by saying they were just doing their jobs. We had choppers flying over the house night and day, and a drone even landed on our skylight. At one stage, I told Deb that I should go downstairs, get a gun, and give the journos and the world media what they wanted—me dead and gone. I thought if I did that, it would all end for my family, then and there. In that moment, Deb realised just how much the media pack had affected my mental health. She had always known me to be incredibly strong and it shocked her that I had come to this point.

I spoke with my family, telling them that I could no longer handle the unrelenting pressure from the media—my head felt as if it was exploding. We were all completely shattered, and we agreed the best decision was for me to resign.

So, seventeen years of blood, sweat and tears came to an end, after I rang Pauline to tell I had decided to resign. I told her I had to . . . for my family's sake and for the sake of the party I'd worked tirelessly for since January the 13th 2017. Candidates and countless members of One Nation had spent a lot of money, time and energy getting ready for the federal election. I knew it didn't matter what the truth was, the media were not going to let this go. It was enough for them that I was a member of One Nation—they wanted blood, so I gave it to them.

When I rang Pauline, she asked how Deb was handling the situation. She is a good person, who really cared about my wife and my family. It was people over the party every time for her. I felt I'd let everybody down—myself, my wife, my family, the One Nation family, and the whole country—it was an enormous weight to carry.

I put out a media release that, unfortunately, had a spelling error in it. The distress I was going through, combined with my dyslexia, didn't do me any favours and the media had a field day at my expense all over again. I didn't think it was possible, but things went from really bloody bad to even worse; it was humiliating and traumatic for everyone.

My media release said:

> To my wife Debbie, my family, Senator Pauline Hanson, the One Nation membership, my friends and the Australian people.
>
> I would like to sincerely apologise for my behaviour that was aired on television last night as a result of the

Al Jazeera covert operation filmed in the United States in September 2018.

The footage shown does not reflect the person I am. It shows a person who was drunk and not in control of his actions and I take full responsibility for allowing that to happen.

I informed my wife Debbie the following morning that I had attended a strip club in Washington DC, and that I had too many drinks and little recollection of the night. She accepted that and after viewing the footage, I am thankful that she is standing by me. Debbie knows that my untoward actions were the result of excessive consumption of alcohol and I am deeply remorseful for the hurt that I have caused her, my family and the people that support me.

I am also deeply remorseful for my disrespectful comments towards women.

I found the footage difficult to watch as my words and actions under intoxication and in that environment, are not a true reflection of myself.

Despite being on a self-funded trip with a person who I never imagined to be an undercover journalist funded by the Qatar government, yesterday I offered Senator Pauline Hanson my resignation.

I will not be conducting any media interviews or making further statements. As I will no longer be of pubic interest, I ask that you please respect my family's privacy at this time.

Steve Dickson.

A diabolical spelling mistake that many have made before me and, no doubt, many will make it after me. Unfortunately mine occurred on a global platform—the print media.

Chapter 36

The bitter pill

I'm normally a very strong person, I'm the man people go to when the shit hits the fan, but this time I was the man, who didn't know what to do or think—I was lost. The days felt like one long, excruciating blur. The media camped outside our front gates around the clock for three days. We had a greater media presence at our home than the man who massacred fifty people in a mosque in New Zealand—it was absurd.

Day and night became one. I was so numb I couldn't differentiate between the two. I couldn't sleep, I couldn't eat, I couldn't function, but I needed to, so I could get a grip on this situation and figure out what had happened, and why.

ACA continued their punishing crusade, with Tracy Grimshaw going for One Nation's jugular. They succeeded. I was dust so they turned their attention to Pauline. *ACA* interviewed Pauline at her property, and it was one the toughest interviews I have seen her endure. Tracey Grimshaw went as far as to say, "Walk away, just walk away". Those of us, who know Pauline, know she would never walk away from the Australian people and would never let someone be unfairly treated.

The week was like an agonising Groundhog Day torturing us over and over again—and it just wouldn't stop. I thank God for Deb, Christian and Zeik and their amazing partners, who provided the strength I needed, to weather this cyclone. I could do little but pray, pray and pray.

Deb was beside herself, as my mental state fell deeper into the depths of despair and depression. She remembers thinking, "Holy moly the strongest person in my life wants to end his life, so it will all go away!" She followed me everywhere I went, and I mean everywhere! I would lie on the bed, curled up for hours, which led to days, because every day was exactly the same as the one before and I knew the following day would be no different.

I felt so alone, and it scares me how close to the reality of suicide I actually was. It was a very real option in my mind; a way to make it all go away. The only thing that stopped me was my amazing family—I couldn't do that to Deb, the boys or my mum.

The fourth day arrived, and I still wasn't eating or sleeping. However, the good news was that there wasn't a media pack on our front lawn when we woke up. All that was left was a single car, hidden at the front of a property, obviously containing someone trying to get a photo of anyone arriving at or leaving the property.

The story was still playing on the TV and it was still in media, but there wasn't the pressure of a full media scrum. They were still desperate for any type of news and the calls and messages kept coming in. Pauline called Deb and said to her, "It's like having a pimple on your arse, pop it and move on, you've done nothing wrong." Deb replied to P (as she called her), "It feels like a carbuncle". At that time, when we were in the thick of it, Deb couldn't see it getting any better—she thought it would inevitably get worse.

Deb really appreciated the call from Pauline and afterwards she thought, "Pauline's been jailed for alleged electoral fraud—and cleared. She's been accused of being naked in public on the front page of the Courier Mail—false. Not to mention everything the media has thrown at her and she still can stand strong. Well then, for God's sake, we'll survive Steve's visit to a bloody strip club!"

Deb was furious, not at me, but at Rodger, Diana and Al Jazeera. She felt an unfounded guilt, as if this whole thing was on her because of her comment to Rodger the day he came to our house, about me living in the Philippines as a teenager and dating a movie star. For some reason Deb felt Rodger and Diana had organised the whole strip club visit as a vindictive way to try to separate us.

She was livid that Diana—another woman—would come into our house, pretending to be someone she wasn't, taking advantage of our hospitality and acting as if she was someone who cared about people. She couldn't understand how 'Diana' could live with herself and thought her lust for money had driven her to try to come between a happily married woman and her husband. In her words, "Real women don't try to destroy such a bond". I couldn't argue with any of it.

In a statement to the media, Deb said, "*I have known the man for 34 years and the person I saw on film was not my husband. He's been to a thousand functions here in Australia and never once has he got rotten drunk. Never in our life together has he ever gone to or even indicated he wanted to go to a strip club, not that I would ever have stopped him from going. Never have I ever seen him so disrespectful towards women. I was shocked and speechless. That is not Steve. In amongst the carnage, my bond with my husband had never been stronger.*"

In hindsight, I wish that I'd never met Rodger Muller or invited him into our world.

What Rodger, Diana and Al Jazeera did to my family was nothing short of an unethical media assassination. Deb and my boys didn't deserve it and neither did I. I was just collateral damage in their master plan to destroy One Nation.

People who watched it play out in the media, but they didn't know me personally, and they didn't understand how much I love and care about my family.

The social media trial and trolls were relentless. It was difficult to read what people were saying—they were keyboard warriors with nothing better to do and they had no concept of what was happening behind our closed doors.

Chapter 37

Foreign interference

After the media circus left town, we had time to rest and a respite from constant scrutiny. That meant we have a greater capacity to think, process, and to gain some balance and direction. As we began the search for answers, we went from asking, 'How?' to 'Why?'

The more we found out about Al Jazeera and their smear campaign, the more questions it raised. We knew that they had spent around three years and millions of dollars filming their two-part documentary, *How to Sell a Massacre* . . . three years! Why would they spend that amount of time and money and then sell it to the ABC, for just $5000 in-kind?

They had put the documentary together and sold it to the ABC conveniently to be aired just before the federal election, to bring down One Nation. Not satisfied with the result (of not burying One Nation with their concocted documentary), they then sat on the strip club sting footage for seven months, before it miraculously appeared on *ACA* just days after my federal nomination for the Senate.

The buck didn't stop with Peter Charley, Rodger Muller, Diana Armatta, and Al Jazeera however. The mainstream media had blood on their hands as well. They grabbed hold of the allegation that James and I flew to the States to ask the NRA for money for our campaign. I did not ask the NRA, or anyone in the USA for that matter, for money.

There's not one bit of footage showing me doing so either, because I didn't! Yet the media would not let it go; they kept making these wildly untrue accusations.

Why did Al Jazeera heavily edit, manipulate and put together a documentary, intended to air just two days after the NSW election, and why did they involve themselves in Australian politics?

How did *ACA* end up with the story showing me at a strip club? Al Jazeera said they were furious that the footage had been *leaked*, but did they feed it or sell it to *ACA*, or was that the ABC?

Why didn't any of the other people filmed in the documentary ever get a phone call from the Australian media? Why weren't they asked whether the footage was real or fabricated or, indeed, what actually happened?

We do know a few things for sure. One of them is that you cannot trust Peter Charley, the journalist who reported in the documentary, as far as you can throw him. He even won a Walkley Award for his unethical journalist piece, as stated by Peter Greste on SBS news, which effectively broke every MEAA rule! I suppose whoever was behind it knew what he was like and that's why he was chosen—he could be counted on to report a heap of garbage.

For us, some simple questions should have been asked about the whole situation, to put it into some kind of perspective.

Have you ever gotten drunk and done or said something stupid or horrible?

I did that once, but you already know that.

Have you ever been to a strip club, or bucks or hen's night where there was a stripper?

Me too; twice in my entire life, but it's not a crime. When he was asked for a statement for this book, Nicholas Triantis, the owner of the strip club that Rodger took me to, said:

"Nobody's allowed to film anything in this club, that's strictly forbidden. There's no private rooms, no lap dancing, anything. I think that was just cherry picked. We're the only club in the country that doesn't have lap dances, private rooms, everything is out in the open. We're the only social club. We've been open for forty years. He (Steve Dickson) came to the most conservative club there is, and this guy (Rodger Muller) just cherry-picked stuff. I could tell. Obviously he'd (Steve) had a few drinks…said what he said…but nothing happened beyond that…he was set up obviously."

A well-planned foreign media sting got me rolling drunk, and asked the right question to get the required answer, all to suit a specific comment in a storyline more fictitious than Harry Potter, in order to interfere with an Australian election. Someone had a lot to fear and a lot to lose by One Nation gaining power.

Overseas money and an overseas media group (Al Jazeera) are behind this sting. Al Jazeera is owned by a foreign government, who openly supports Islamic terror organisations that are banned in Australia. So, was this great con job the brainchild of Al Jazeera or was it hatched on Australian soil?

What I did is a crime against my own values and my commitment to my family and I've faced the punishment and ridicule that resulted from that stupid act . . .

. . . what Peter and Rodger and their team did is also likely a crime, under Division 92 of the Foreign Interference Act.

They collaborated with a foreign government and its media company, intentionally to interfere with an Australian election. If convicted, Mr Muller and his mates rightly face imprisonment for twenty years.

If Australians have collaborated with supporters of an Islamic terrorist group, with the sole purpose of interfering with an Australian election, then I want to ask why the government and the Australian Federal Police (AFP) haven't acted on this.

Why haven't they investigated my complaints and charged people? It's not as though there's no readily available evidence—it played on our TVs night after night!

The AFP and federal government already know that:

1. Mr Muller and his associates were funded and supported by a foreign- government-owned media company, whose intent was to interfere with our election. Peter Charley admitted this in an interview. Fact.

2. Al Jazeera paid Rodger Muller to spy on the Australian political party where I was a member. Fact.

3. Al Jazeera paid Rodger Muller to dig dirt, and when he couldn't find any, they helped him create dirt. When Muller found no connection between One Nation and the American Gun Lobby, Al Jazeera money enabled him to organise meetings to try and create connections. Fact.

4. When I didn't ask for money from the American Gun Lobby, Al Jazeera paid Rodger and his associates to lie and edit video footage to make it appear as though One Nation had asked the NRA for money. Fact.

5. The same foreign money, which helps support Islamic terrorists, also helped Muller, and his friends in the Australian

media, sit on this footage for seven months and then release it just before the 2019 election. Fact.

Has Australia become a country where the federal law enforcement authorities can turn a blind eye to serious crimes, because doing so might be helpful to the political party in power?

We will find out over the coming months. I have a secret report from the AFP, which shows that they *know* our Foreign Interference laws (see below) were most likely broken.

The AFP *knows* a proper investigation is warranted, in order to explain how millions of dollars—from a country that supports Islamic terror—were used to fund a three-year media sting, deliberately designed to interfere with an Australian election. However, the AFP is no different to many other government anti-corruption bodies. They understand that if you don't ask the questions, you won't hear the evil.

Division 92—Foreign interference

Subdivision A—Preliminary

92.1 Definitions

In this Division:

deception means an intentional or reckless deception, whether by words or other conduct, and whether as to fact or as to law, and includes:

(a) a deception as to the intentions of the person using the deception or any other person; and

(b) conduct by a person that causes a computer, a machine or an electronic device to make a response that the person is not authorised to cause it to do.

Menaces has the same meaning as in Part 7.5 (see section 138.2).

Subdivision B—Foreign interference

92.2 Offence of intentional foreign interference

Interference generally

(1) A person commits and offence if:

    (a) the person engages in conduct; and

    (b) any of the following circumstances exists:

        (i) the person engages in the conduct on behalf of, or in collaboration with, a foreign principal or a person acting on behalf of a foreign principal;

        (ii) the conduct is directed, funded or supervised by a foreign principal or a person acting on behalf of a foreign principal; and

    (c) the person intends that the conduct will:

        (i) influence a political or government process of the Commonwealth or a State or Territory; or

        (ii) influence the exercise (whether or not in Australia) of an Australian democratic or political right or duty; or

        (iii) support intelligence activities of a foreign principal; or

        (iv) prejudice Australia's national security; and

    (d) any part of the conduct:

        (i) is covert or involves deception; or

        (ii) involves the person making a threat to cause serious harm, whether to the person to whom the threat is made or any other person; or

        (iii) involves the person making a demand with menaces.

Penalty: Imprisonment for 20 years

92.3 Offence of reckless foreign interference

Interference generally

   (1) A person commits an offence if:

      (a) the person engages in conduct; and

      (b) any of the following circumstances exists:

         (i) the conduct is engaged on behalf of, or in collaboration with, a foreign principal or a person acting on behalf of a foreign principal;

         (ii) the conduct is directed, funded or supervised by a foreign principal or a person acting on behalf of a foreign principal; and

      (c) the person is reckless as to whether the conduct will:

         (i) influence a political or governmental process of the Commonwealth or a State or Territory; or

         (ii) influence the exercise (whether or not in Australia) or an Australian democratic or political right or duty ; or

         (iii) support intelligence activities or a foreign principal; or

         (iv) prejudice Australia's national security; and

      (d) any part of the conduct:

         (i) is covert or involves deception; or

         (ii) involves the person making a threat to cause serious harm, whether to the person to whom the threat is made or any other person; or

         (iii) involves the person making a demand with menaces.

   Penalty: Imprisonment for 15 years.

Chapter 38

Recovery and research

Deb and I began talking about what was next for us. We discussed what we should do, and how our life should look and be in the aftermath of the war Al Jazeera had waged against us.

With no job and still feeling devastated, we discussed selling up and taking off to Tasmania to begin a new life there. I'm not the greatest fan of the cold but that seemed preferable to living with the relentless media attention. I questioned whether we could withstand the damage done to our lives here. We were concerned about how we would be perceived in our own community. Looking back, it is clear we were going through the full grieving process and had arrived at the fight or flight stage.

Eventually, things settled down a bit and after talking to the many people, who phoned us or stopped out the front of our house when we were gardening, we could see a common thread in what they said, "Anyone could see you were totally set up".

While the ignorant keyboard warriors continued their ill-informed rants, every person, with whom we had face-to-face contact, was disgusted, and shocked, and thought it shameful that someone would go to those lengths to remove me from politics.

Hearing their kind words of support helped us reconnect with our community. It took Deb three months to get back out there, but for me the bruising didn't start to fade until around the ten-month mark.

Then, with the help of our dear friend, Esther, I took those first small steps back into life. I'll always be grateful to her for helping prop us up when we dropped in a heap.

Getting back out there into the real world included talking about the setup and Al Jazeera. At first people must have thought we'd lost our minds; this didn't happen to people like us! However, the more we spoke out in the public arena and told the true story of what had happened to our family, the more empowered we felt about telling the world the truth.

Truth is everything to us and always will be. You have two options in life: sit back and cop it, or stand up and fight for yourself.

Feeling better and stronger, we started digging for some serious answers. Who was Rodger Muller? Who was Peter Charley? Who was Diana Armatta? We began with a Google search and found Muller's real name really was Rodger Muller. This was confirmed in several articles, including one about his wife Alison, who had been charged and found guilty of fraud. image 62

On December the 16th 2019, the South Coast Register reported that Alison Muller had scammed her employee and even gave a couple of 'stolen' thousand dollars to none other than her husband, Rodger Muller.

> A Woodhill women found guilty of defrauding a series of Nowra, turf companies of more than $180,000 has avoided time behind bars. Instead Alison Louise Muller, 49, has been placed on an 18-month intensive corrections order, meaning she can serve her sentence in the community.

In Burwood Local Court on Friday (December 13) Magistrate Alison Viney also ordered she undertake 350 hours and in one case pay compensation of $1777.

Alison Muller originally pleaded not guilty to 11 charges of dishonestly obtaining financial advantage by deception and one of publishing misleading material to obtain deception.

Magistrate Viney found her guilty of 11 charges after a number of special court sittings in Nowra, Milton and Sydney.

Each offence carries a maximum 10 years jail sentence.

Muller's husband Rodger, a Shoalhaven Heads businessman, sensationally shot to fame earlier this year when it was revealed he had spent years undercover for Al Jazeera exposing both One Nation and America's National Rifle Association.

Police alleged Alison was working for a number of businesses all owned by Gavin Rogers, when she either overpaid herself as an employee or transferred money to her own company or onto her credit card on multiple occasions between February 2010 and April 2014.

Court papers revealed Alison Muller transferred money ($2750) onto her husband's credit card.

What a piece of work these two were! We found articles about him being thrown out of an awards' night for making derogatory remarks. The more we dug; the uglier the facts got. Many locals in his area contacted us and none of what they had to say about Muller was flattering. If we had managed to find all this out, then surely if the media were actually interested in reporting the truth, they only needed to take a quick trip to his local and ask the right questions.

Rodger Muller has been portrayed to the entire world as the hero that saved us all from One Nation. One has to wonder why we haven't heard a word from him since. Where is he? Who is he working for? Someone whom the media believed without question has mysteriously vanished!

To keep our minds off all that happened, Deb and I have got stuck into new projects in our yard. We have built new paths, used second-hand posi tracks to make a fantastic looking garden edge and have planted a vegetable garden. It was a great winter for crops and we have had a bounty of tomatoes, corn, cabbage, peas and broccoli. Growing edible plants is wonderfully rewarding but it can also be challenging, when you rely on natural deterrents, so our native bees aren't exposed to chemicals.

Exercise has been another great way out of the black hole I fell into. Christian got me into a strenuous training program, three days a week, and he pushes me as hard as he can to make me stronger and more resilient. It's hard yakka, but it's something I've really enjoyed. The old saying, 'healthy body, healthy mind' is actually spot on. My mental health is improving, because my body is healthier.

Chapter 39

The Covid campaign

I had been a homebody for almost a year and rarely left our property, other than for the few community events that I'd lent a hand with, in particular the Buderim-Palmwoods Heritage Tramway Inc. meetings.

For a number of years, the group has been making a big push for the Krauss locomotive to be placed in Buderim, but the local councillor would not support it in any way. The train should be housed in Buderim Central; it's a piece of Buderim's history that belongs in our town. The same councillor was a major player in the destruction of the town's beloved Urban Food Street, the one that I took Pauline on a tour of. The councillor didn't get on with the fellow who started the Urban Food Street. They continually butted heads and, sadly, their feud played a large part in eight-year old fruit trees being cut off at ground level, which only inflamed the relationship further.

These were two major community causes about which I felt extremely passionate. So, at the instigation of several community members, and with lots of encouragement from Deb, I contemplated going back into local government, to help these people out. On January the 29th 2020, Deb put up the $10k for my campaign. Despite everything I have put her through, she is still my rock and number one supporter. I took a deep breath and announced my intention to run for Division 7 in the local government area of the Sunshine Coast.

If I said the campaign was really tough, I'd be understating it. It was exceptionally challenging.

I copped a lot of flack from both the media and some community members. I'd bought 300 corflute signs and every night a heap went missing; some with their timber stakes still attached, others with the sign pulled off of it and the stake left sitting bare in the ground.

It wasn't just my signs that went missing. A mystery moped rider, who was delivering brochures for the opposition, was stealing my brochures from mailboxes. We caught two twenty-year olds, on CCTV, throwing eggs at our house. Fortunately, our home is a good 50 metres from the front gate and their reach didn't quite make the distance. It goes to show you the lengths some people will go to, but this was nothing compared to what I'd already been, through. It was disappointing more than anything, especially for Deb who had funded it all.

On the lighter side of the campaign, some of our signs that were taken reappeared transformed into superhero signs such as the Flash, Batman and Spiderman. There are some talented artists on the Sunshine Coast and their work brought a smile to our faces and gave us a great laugh. You get so used to negativity and then the sun shines through, with people who make you smile. We truly do have a great community here.

I forged ahead, working day and night; determined to give it my all. The support I had was overwhelming and over 100 people volunteered to hand out 'how to vote' cards on election day. I was overjoyed; things were looking pretty good.

Two people that stood out were Marie and Noel. They were there every step of the way—coming to local markets with me on Sundays, and walking around wearing my T-shirts that had 'Vote1 Steve Dickson' emblazoned on the front of them. They wore them everywhere! There was no question about whom they were supporting and it inspired me to do my absolute best every day. I was truly appreciative of their support.

In our first week of pre-polling, beginning on March the 20th, the coronavirus (COVID-19) ramped up in Australia, and we weren't permitted to have the volunteers at polling booths as planned. I thought it was a good decision; I didn't want them putting their lives at risk for an election campaign.

Fortunately, the government stopped everyone from handing out 'how to vote' cards, so we were all on a level playing field. I believe the government should have just put 'how to vote' cards inside each polling booth, so people could make their own minds up about whom they wished to vote for, and how to do that. It would have been so much better than running the gauntlet, which as we all know is a daunting prospect for most people these days. It would have also eliminated the huge waste of paper that you get at every election.

One week later, the election was all over. Only 70% of residents voted, because of the virus, and I ended up achieving about 20% of the vote, which I was genuinely happy with, considering the bad publicity I'd received over the past year.

The whisper campaign had definitely affected my result, but I understood it—many people believed the lies told by the media, Al Jazeera and *A Current Affair*. Why wouldn't they! They didn't know the true story so what else could they believe.

Chapter 40

Setting the record straight

I'd been discussing the idea of writing a book with Deb. I wanted to tell my story and to put the rumours to bed, by having it all on the record, but without its being corrupted or edited to suit the media's agenda. After the election and the flack I copped, I knew that now was the right time. Writing a book as a person with dyslexic was always going to be a challenge, but with the encouragement and help of an author friend I began.

Around the same time, on February the 27th 2020, I made an official complaint to the AFP, regarding what I, and several others I'd spoken to, suspected to be political interference by Al Jazeera and the ACA.

Deb and I met with the federal police; two of whom came to our house and interviewed us extensively for about an hour. I'd become cagey since the Al Jazeera and Rodger Muller situation, so I asked them if I could record it—I was not about to take any chances of being taken out of context again. They gave their permission and I gave them a step-by-step account of every single thing I did and said, and how it happened. I gave them all the information I had discovered since the footage was aired, and explanations and data of why it was a case of suspected political interference by a foreign country.

1. This whole affair was instigated and paid for by Al Jazeera, which is fully owned and run by the Qatari royal family, who also run the government of Qatar.

2. Rodger Muller and Peter Charley are employed by Al Jazeera; they pretended to be part of a group called Gun Rights Australia.

3. They approached One Nation to infiltrate, set up and sting the party and its representatives.

4. They planned and created meetings for One Nation representatives in the USA, and they secretly videoed and voice recorded all the movement that they had organised.

5. They fabricated a story, after finding no links between One Nation and any USA companies or organisations; this all happened in September 2018.

6. They released their secret video recording to the ABC, on March the 25th and 27th 2019, six months after the footage was taken. Why?

7. The federal election was announced on April the 11th 2019, and rolls closed for the election on April the 18th. Nominations closed for party candidates on April the 21st, and all nominations closed on April the 23rd. The declaration of candidate nominations was on April the 24th, voting commenced on April the 29th, and the election was held on May the 18th 2019. The dates prove that it was a case of suspected political interference that affected the outcome of a federal election.

8. On April the 30th 2019, Al Jazeera released a statement on *TV Tonight*, which said:

"Al Jazeera said the footage from the strip club had been used without the network's permission. The material was gathered, but a decision was made by Al Jazeera not to broadcast it as part of the investigation", said Phil Rees, head of investigations at the outlet.

> "Al Jazeera did not consider it was in the public interest to broad cast the material... Al Jazeera condemns the unathorized use of its material."

So, the following questions remain. How did *ACA* acquire the strip club footage and why hasn't Al Jazeera taken action against *ACA* for using their footage? Surely, Dan Nolan, the producer of *ACA* and a former employee of Al Jazeera, would have known what their stance would be on using unauthorised footage!

This footage was intentionally aired at the most critical time (five days after nominations had closed for the federal election) to cause the *greatest* amount of damage to One Nation as possible, and the powers that be knew that.

I received an email from the AFP on the morning of August the 14th 2020. It was classified as 'PROTECTED AND SENSITIVE'.

I replied to them, regarding the content (which I am not permitted to disclose) via email, on August the 14th, and again on August the 30th. I asked for additional information about my complaint, but I have yet to receive confirmation that it will be investigated. I also asked if I could release the findings they sent me in the email.

On August the 30th, I received a response from the AFP saying that the contents of the email were for 'Official use only', which effectively prevents me from showing it to anyone, talking about it, or writing about it.

On September the 1st, I made contact with an AFP representative, who reiterated the above.

> Protected—level 3. High business impact=damage to the national interest, organisations or individuals
>
> Sensitive—level 2. Low to medium business impact=limited damage to an individual, organisation or government generally if compromised

It is clear that none of this happened by accident. It was all meticulously planned and staged by Rodger Muller and Al Jazeera, with the assistance of Claudianna Blanca, and Peter Charley. Although the AFP have silenced me for the time being, I will not give up on my search to unearth the truth of what happened and why. I will not rest until those involved have been held accountable for what they did to my life.

Chapter 41

Bouncing back

It was twelve months since I had done any national TV. I'd declined every invitation I received. It took me almost a year, after the Al Jazeera story went to air on Channel 9, to overcome the depression and to rebuild my self-esteem and confidence. I have poured the majority of my energy into my recovery, and into being there for my family and rebuilding our lives.

I have taken a long hard look at myself and done a fair bit of soul searching, to determine if I had anything else of value to contribute to my community. I realised I still had a strong desire to help and to go into bat for those wanting to be heard and helped.

Writing this book has helped me face a few truths and fears. It was productive in the process of healing and moving on. I discovered a lot about myself—one thing being that I was not done and dusted. I have more to give and am capable of delivering on it.

When Peter Gleeson from Sky News invited me to do an interview with him, I was ready to get back out there . . . nervous, but ready. On May the 6th 2020, I drove to Brisbane, listening to music on the way to clear my mind and to relax. By the time I arrived, I was more than ready. image 64

After I arrived at Sky News' Bowen Hills studio, I walked into the building and was signing in and going over the Covid-19 entry protocol, when Deb Frecklington (QLD LNP leader) and her entourage came through the front door.

We were both surprised to see each other. Deb had no choice but to acknowledge me, luckily she didn't need to shake my hand as contact was banned under the Covid-19 protocol I had just read through. I wouldn't have had a problem with it though. Deb was pleasant enough, but I got the feeling she didn't like the idea of me being back on her turf.

Peter asked me a barrage of questions as respectfully as he could. Some were confronting, but all of them fathomable—and the first of them was about the impact the Al Jazeera piece had on me. My response was, "Well Peter, it's been almost one year to the day that it all occurred. A Middle Eastern media outlet—Al Jazeera—paid two undercover agents to make up a story that would affect the federal election. They surely succeeded at that. I went to a strip club and got drunk and said some foolish things that men do sometimes, just like Kevin Rudd and a number of other politicians, but of course I made a mistake of going to the pub with a bloke who was on a mission to destroy One Nation."

I had made a firm decision not to be pulled in by only talking about the Al Jazeera stuff. There were more important issues happening around the country to talk about.

"We are facing a pandemic that's destroying our economy, and killing people" I said.

Then, Peter asked me about China and what my thoughts were about where the coronavirus had come from and that the implications of that were. I said, "The word compensation comes to mind. China should be paying compensation to the rest of the world."

"Either the coronavirus came from a wet market or a biological centre. One of three things could have happened: it could have from the wet market, or it could have been an accidental escape from the biological centre at Wuhan, or it might have been intentionally released."

I added, "on the middle ground; let's say it escaped from the Wuhan biological centre, and if so, the fact that the Chinese government had kept its existence secret for a number of weeks, before telling the rest of the world that it existed at all, proves that their truth is problematic."

He asked what I thought about the economy and how we could fix it. I said, "Australians need cheap energy and cheap water. They should both be considered as essential services. Business would flourish, and jobs would be created, and a hybrid of the Bradfield Scheme, which I took to the 2017 state election as a policy, would drought-proof Australia. This in turn would open up opportunities for growth. The middle of Australia is barren and dry, and the land is almost valueless. If you added water to the land, you would add value to the land, which would create the opportunity to build cities, farms, manufacturing, agriculture, and environmental reserves. The land would become a major asset for the future. We must also build power stations: coal, nuclear, hydrogen, solar, wind, or anything that will create cheap energy, but it has to be owned by government and sold at cost."

Peter also asked me if I was thinking of running at the next state election. I said, "Funny you should ask that question" as Michael McKenna, a journalist, had asked me the same question five minutes before I went to air. I said, "I'm thinking about it, but haven't made a decision either way".

Peter wrapped up the interview by asking what I had been up to. I told him I was writing a book and hopeful it would be out by the end of the year.

Interview done, I was relieved it went well and I got to talk about issues I found important. I posted the Sky News story on my Facebook the next day, and got a positive reaction to it with 413 likes, 232 comments and 45 shares. Clearly, what I had spoken about had struck a nerve.

Many people commented that I had very strong views and all condemned China for not taking full responsibility for the virus' spreading beyond their borders.

"As a business owner, if I impact on other people due to my negligence, I know that I would expect legal issues and ultimately have an obligation to make good."

"Absolutely yes! China needs to compensate every country affected by the virus."

A few days later Deb and I spoke about what was next for me. I said I was keen to get back in the saddle and to run for state government, in the October election. Deb's initial reaction was panic. She couldn't think about anything else other than the media harassment happening all over again. She wondered if we were strong enough to run the gauntlet, again. She hoped the book would be out before the election, and the true story would finally set the record straight. She wanted people to know and understand our family, what our values were, the integrity we have, and how committed we are to our family and to our community.

She pondered the idea for a while, before coming to me and saying she knew I had only ever strived to do the right thing by people and that had dedicated seventeen years of my life to doing that and doing it well. She said she was extremely proud of my achievements and the difference I had made, and that my desire to help was still there in abundance, so she would support me fully in my run for state election.

Deb was nervous and I couldn't blame her, but as she said in an interview, "Steve loves the Sunshine Coast. In my heart I know it's what he's meant to be doing. He cares so much and has absolutely no self-interest; everything he does he does for the community, what they want. I'm so proud of him and couldn't say no to someone I love so much, and who is so passionate—it was a definite yes from me."

Before making my final decision, I spoke to Christian and Zeik, and to some of my close friends to get their thoughts on my running in the October election. Each gave me considered advice as we went through the range of challenges that I may or may not come up against. It was brilliant counsel and I valued it entirely.

Fortunately, the March local election had been a sort of dry run and had helped to build my confidence to do the job and do it well. I had bucket loads of experience, energy and a determination to be the voice the community needed to get things done. I knew I could leave a positive footprint and a legacy for my community and family, but first I had to get in there and WIN!

I was excited by the prospect of ensuring our beloved Sunshine Coast does not become another sprawling high-density Gold Coast. It is my family's home. Our roots are imbedded deep into Sunny Coast soil. I know the decisions being made now will have a great impact on what our region will look like in ten years. We need someone in government, who isn't just going to be a party puppet but who is prepared to fight.

I am used to going against the grain and know I have the right insight and contacts to make a difference.

On August the 12th, I took a deep breath and went public with my intention of running *and* winning the state seat of Buderim; this time as an independent.

The Sunshine Coast news announced that all the parties, with the exception of the Greens (One Nation, the ALP and the LNP) had nominated a candidate in my area.

There are no other independents, but I believe a genuine independent candidate could have a real chance. In fact, I feel that an independent is exactly what the community needs, as there are no party agendas to adhere to. With seventeen years of experience, I know the ins and outs and I know I can deliver the best outcomes, without being attached to a party.

I've achieved a lot in my political career, but there are still a number of unfinished items on my 'to do' list. I've been out talking with the community, and informing myself about what is important to them and what is needed. Common issues are high on their priority list, such as homelessness, job creation, new industry opportunities, and drought and bushfire issues. These are all achievable; we just need the right politicians to be vocal about them, to push for them and to fight for their local communities.

The journey is well underway, now. Conversations are being had, the election marketing has begun, and I'm out collecting data and feedback from the public. I'm printing corflute signs, organising mail outs, doing videos, and talking about real issues on my social media pages. I am excited about the campaign and the upcoming election.

The policies I'll be championing are:

- The implementation of a hybrid of the Bradfield Scheme, to drought-proof Australia, finally. It's a project that would create long-term jobs in the building phase and which would add value to land that is almost worthless without water. Cities could be built, farming land established, as well as forests for the environment and the timber industry. The opportunities are almost endless.

- Change laws to protect Australian interests in essential services, in and industry. Cut the red and green tape that is strangling farmers and industry alike.

- Ensure all land ownership in the country is at least 51% Australian, thereby protecting our assets and preserving our children's future with the same ownership laws that are in place in other countries throughout the world.

- A Citizen Initiated Referenda—giving people the right to put ideas forward at elections and which, if supported by the majority, could be voted on now, at a federal election and which could become law if approved by the public.

- Allow medicinal cannabis to be prescribed by physicians and sold over the counter at chemists.

- Build more coal-fired power stations—everyone agrees with alternative energy sources, such as solar and wind, but we needed base load energy to power our economy, so that manufacturing can prosper again in our country. Without cheap reliable electricity, Australia will continue to lose its place as the manufacturer we once were.

- Tax multinationals, which currently pay little or no tax at all; thereby, treating all Australians equally. This extra money could be used to build dams and power stations, and to protect the environment, create jobs, pay back Australia's spiralling debt and more.

- Cut back on immigration. At this stage, Australia can no longer support extra immigrants, who affect our roads, hospitals, welfare, school, jobs, etc. We need to change our thinking completely on this.

- Form a better relationship with the USA. The world is becoming more unstable as each day passes. As the Chinese government infiltrates the South-Pacific region and builds military bases in the South China Sea, we must re-establish strong relationships with the USA.

- Call out China for its intrusion into the South China Sea. Australia needs to push back against the Chinese government's military build-up, given their potential threat to our ongoing fuel supplies from Singapore.

- Deliver a number of initiatives for the State Electorate of Buderim: i.e. free public transport, small business transition programs, sustainable growth, cheap electricity, cheap water, a number of sporting and community buildings, the MRI (Mooloola River Interchange), an entertainment centre and the heavy rail.

As each day passes, I see our sovereignty diminishing. People are losing faith in our politicians at all levels of government. They no longer trust the United Nations or the European Union and with good reason. Even fishermen can't make a living in a country surrounded by water—the rules and regulations are crippling them.

Industries such as car manufacturing no longer exist in this great country. The next to go will be our aluminium smelters, as the cost of electricity is certain to force them offshore into countries that have cheaper energy, such as China or India.

In my conversations with Queenslanders, I've found that people are more than aware of the problems we are all facing. However, the biggest problem seems to be that Queenslanders, indeed most Australians, have no faith in our leaders anymore.

Where did it all go wrong? I believe that the voting system is broken. When locally elected representatives tow the party line, rather than support their electorate, you know we are in trouble. Things need to change, and I'd like to help make Australia a better, stronger and more self-reliant country.

Chapter 42

Reflection

My life has definitely been colourful and before I quit, I intend on adding a few more brighter, happier colours to my palette.

I have weathered a storm I should never have been in the middle of. I know that if I hadn't joined One Nation, none of this would have happened to me. Perhaps some other, unsuspecting fellow would have been caught up in it instead. We'll never know!

The problem we face in Australia is that the truth no longer counts. Some journalists still believe in ethical journalism but, sadly, they are now out-numbered by the unethical tabloid style of journalism—anything for a rating, like or share.

The MEAA has also lost its way, in its support of those who break every code within its own organisation. The Walkley Awards effectively became valueless, after unethical journalism won the award.

I hope that my experience will never be repeated by anyone else in this great country. I hope that true journalism will prevail, and will fight through the muck, fluff and dribble to get its head above water delivering stories that matter—with truth and integrity.

I'm not bitter anymore. I've been there and done that, and I have spent too many hours wallowing in it. None of this happened by accident. It put me through the wringer of life, but it taught me lessons that I wouldn't have learnt otherwise.

I don't blame One Nation; I blame myself for not being astute enough to walk my own path. I've learned.

Do I want justice? Hell, yes! But, it doesn't consume me and if it doesn't come I won't lose any sleep over it. I am moving forward. I will continue to love my wife and my family. I will work hard and do what I feel is my calling in life—assisting as many fellow residents as I humanly can. I'll fight for the ones who are weary from their fight, and stand up for those who can't and be the voice of those who have shouted so long they now whisper.

A few scars build character. This journey has proven to me that even on the worst day of your life, the sun comes up in the morning, and you can still get up to smile. You can live to your greatest capacity and fulfil your life's purpose.

Releasing this book is my closure. I can put the past to bed and open a new book to create a story that has a bright future full of colour.

And that's what I intend to do . . .

Acknowledgements

Deb and I would like to thank those who cared, called, emailed, texted and cried with us in our hours of need.

There are so many people that I can't write all their names here—family, friends, and politicians from all parties. There are even some from the media, who were disgusted with the unethical journalism.

I want to single out my beautiful wife Deb; my son Christian and his partner Samantha, my son Zeik and his partner Heeyoung. Thank you, you saved my life when the black dog was biting at my ankles. I can't thank you enough; I love you.

My fabulous sister, Teresa, and my beautiful mother, Joan, have always been there offering their love and support.

Special thanks also to our good friend Esther, who never stopped supporting us in the good times and the bad—she is an amazing lady, who pushed me beyond what I thought was possible, Deb and I will always be truly grateful. Small steps at first but move forward we did, with your help.

There's Alan Jones, whom I've learned a lot from and who I admire immensely. He and is generously lending his support for my book launch. Alan is a true patriotic Australian champion. He calls a spade a spade; says life's too short for bullshit, and has never been afraid to speak his mind. He puts up a good fight to prevent evil from prevailing.

He's always cheered me on, even wearing a shirt for the 2017 election emblazoned with, 'I'm sticking with Steve' on the front! Like I said; a real champion whom I appreciate.

Lastly, Deb and I would like to thank, Gino, Marie, Laurence, Donna, Russell, Rodger F, Josh, Anna, Jeannine, Grant, Andrew, Dave, Kerry, Shane, Shannon, Noel, Maxina, Gibbo, James, Ken, Murray, Sheree, Rob, Fern, Christine, Darren, Margaret, Alan, Sandra, Colin, Dennis, Barry, Mark, Phil, Becky, Alistair and Rachael. To any I have missed, you know I will be forever grateful for your love and support.

To you the reader—thank you for buying my book and spending some time reading it. I truly hope you have enjoyed it and know a little more about me now, as well as the dirty world of the media and government.

Knowledge is power, may the wisdom you now have support the good eggs, and keep the rotten ones accountable.

Steve and Deb.

Biography

Born a Queenslander in 1962, Steve Dickson has two sons and lives with Debbie, his beautiful wife of 34 years, on the Sunshine Coast.

An advocate of community, he has dedicated seventeen years to Queensland politics, championing the underdog and fighting to preserve the Australia's great culture and lifestyle.

Follow and connect with Steve on Facebook @SteveDicksonQLD

Website links

National Security Legislation Amendment (Espionage and Foreign Interference) Act 2018. 2018. Accessed September 25, 2020. https://www.legislation.gov.au/Details/C2018A00067.

Photo references

The Morning Bulletin, 16 Feb 2013

South Burnett, 19 June 2014

Sports Grant - https://southburnett.com.au/news2/2014/06/19/sports-projects-get-a-tick/

Redland City – Redland City Bulletin, 29 May 2015
https://www.redlandcitybulletin.com.au/story/3112253/wellington-pt-misses-out-on-reef/

I'm with Steve – Brisbane Times 26 Nov 2017

SBS, 26 March 2019

Pauline Hanson and Steve Dickson – Lisa Marie Williams – Getty Images

Congressional Sportsman dinner photo by Al Jazeera featured on ABC news - https://www.abc.net.au/news/2019-03-26/one-nation-at-congress-sportsmen-event/10939566?nw=0

Sunshine Coast Daily, 13 Aug 2020 https://www.sunshinecoastdaily.com.au/news/how-hellish-ordeal-inspired-dicksons-state-electio/4077787/

www.ingramcontent.com/pod-product-compliance
Lightning Source LLC
Chambersburg PA
CBHW062026290426
44108CB00025B/2792